20
GAME CHANGERS
IN HISTORY
(Series 1)

*A NOTE ON THE LIVES AND
IMPACT OF THESE GREAT MINDS
& HISTORICAL FIGURES*

*(EDISON, FREUD, MOZART, JOAN OF
ARC, JESUS, GANDHI, EINSTEIN,
BUDDHA, AND MORE)*

BY PATRICK MARCUS

D1522685

PATRICK MARCUS

ISBN: 9798838646477

SPECIAL BONUS

Want the Audiobook + this bonus book for Free?

Audiobook

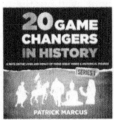

Bonus E-Book

Join the Community and get the Audiobook Version for Free + this Bonus Book

SCAN WITH YOUR PHONE CAMERA

Table of Contents

PATRICK MARCUS

.

INTRODUCTION

When did history become a fact-retaining exercise and stop becoming what it is, our story? To me, what's most important is NOT knowing the exact dates and specific locations but learning about the adversity and sometimes deleterious circumstances these great figures had to fight through. In a time period when there was nowhere near as much technology as there is today, these people still prevailed and changed the world despite all their adversities and setbacks.

It is the story that is interesting, not the facts. And it is the story, not the dates and names, that make history, history. Their stories are meant to inspire you and provide you, the reader, with a new perspective, hopefully aiding you in the fight against whatever challenges you may be facing. No matter who you are, what background you have, or what area of expertise you are interested in, one or more of these historical figures, by example alone, are bound to light a fire in you.

This series contains the stories of rulers, emperors, great minds of philosophy, AND scientific inventors. There are also mythical or mystical figures, religious figures, holocaust survivors and victims, amazing artists, and also some great con-artists. I have also included some of their most thought-provoking and inspirational quotes. Indeed, some of the figures in these books were evil rulers or tricksters, and you should not misconstrue their stories as encouragement to literally follow in their footsteps. Instead, focus on how they succeeded, not necessarily what they accomplished, which were often astonishing achievements. You may also learn some unique and surprising character traits that are not well-known. These figures were often just ordinary people from humble backgrounds with flaws just like you and me.

I truly am astounded by how little people, especially those under the age of 40, know about some of these legendary historical figures. That's the world we live in today. Smartphones and social media. A constant flow of everyone else's activities and information coming onto your screen. Combine all this with the constant bombardment of advertisements and marketing strategies etc., and you are left with people whose attention span has shrunk to that of a toddler.

Another problem is for anyone who does want to learn about key historical figures, there are many books and documentaries about each figure, but oftentimes it is too much information. A book about Napoleon or Nelson Mandela could be hundreds of pages long, filled with dates and details, and descriptions that are just too much information for the millennial and younger generation.

That's why the aim of this book is to give short, concise snippets and synopsis of a variety of unique historical figures. Excitingly telling their stories from a different angle. Pinpointing what they actually achieved and how it can inspire you without getting too bogged down on the finite details and dates and so forth. This is unfortunately why the subject of HISTORY is so hated in secondary and high schools across the world. As a former maths teacher who worked in many schools in different countries, I saw this time and time again. Even when I was in school this was the case. History teachers who are excited and passionate about teaching these stories are shocked at how uninterested and bored 15-year-olds are when in class. All of this is due to a flawed system with textbooks filled with hundreds and hundreds of pages of dates and place names and details, which often kills any enthusiasm a student might have. Of course, I am generalizing here. There is undoubtedly many very keen and interested students and great teachers too.

I'm sure there are many young people out there in their 20s, 30s, or older who would love to know these stories and are maybe even embarrassed that they don't already know about some of these household names. My father used to roll his eyes and look at me with amazement when he would be talking about a famous ruler, and I would say I have never heard of him. So when I did seek to learn more, he would hand me four huge thick books about them. Needless to say, this method never worked. All I wanted was a brief summary and then, in my own time, to learn more.

You will notice I matched up characters from series 1 to series 2 as best I could. For example, the first character, Thomas Edison, is matched up with Nikola Tesla in series 2. Jung is the second character in series 2, opposite Freud in series 1, his predecessor. Then Marcus Aurelius (series 2) came after Caesar (series 1). They do not all correlate but I feel it gives a good dynamic to the series.

This Audiobook and eBook series is meant for everyone of all ages and walks of life to get a glimpse of the mind-blowing stories and achievements of these hugely influential figures who changed the game and the world. My goal is that someone in this book can inspire you in some way or another. Enjoy!

CHAPTER 1

Thomas Edison
(1847-1931)

Inventor of the Light Bulb and the Phonograph

"Our greatest weakness lies in giving up. The most certain way to succeed is always to try just one more time."

- *Thomas Edison*

To the surprise of those who learned about his genius in school, Edison was as much a businessman as he was an inventor. In fact, Thomas Edison is even accused of stealing inventions or concepts and reworking them into a more lucrative asset. He made this admission himself, saying:

"Everybody steals in commerce and industry. I've stolen a lot myself. But I know how to steal."

It should be noted that this quote was paraphrased by a magazine writer who heard Edison say this after confronting him about an alleged commercial theft. However, the quote alone tells a drastically different story than the one we're taught in school—the vision of a genius inventor who created the light bulb after failing 10,000 times. Bottom line, there's a lot you don't know about Thomas Edison. The man has many great accomplishments under his oversized belt, some you probably aren't aware of. He also bears many controversies, especially regarding his famous rivalry with Nikola Tesla.

Early Life
Before the light bulb sparked to life or the phonograph brought music to the masses, Edison could be found in Milan, Ohio, where the genius officially entered the world in 1847 on February 11th. For such a remarkable person, Edison's upbringing was relatively normal.

Except for a few things.

For starters, Thomas Edison was an uncooperative and thus unsuccessful student. After Edison's moving to Port Huron in Michigan his mother decided enough was enough and took him out of school and homeschooled the young hyperactive child. Edison's apparent rebelliousness was in part due to his genetics. His father was an exiled political activist from Canada, indicating that a brash disregard for the rules had been handed down to the young Thomas Edison, foreshadowing the man he would soon become.

Another contributing factor to Edison's struggle with school was a possible case of Attention Deficit Disorder, also known as ADHD. Having such an overactive brain, Edison probably found traditional tedious schoolwork boring. Edison only attended the Port Huron school for 12 weeks before his mother took him out. Fortunately, Edison's mother was a trained educator and allowed Edison to learn at his own pace, which was probably pretty fast and erratic.

This parental decision would prove to be a wise choice. Later on in his childhood, at the age of 12, Edison began showing signs of an entrepreneurial spirit, as well as a knack for experimenting. It all began when Edison started selling newspapers in his local area (a common form of work for young boys in those days). Due to Edison's access to the news bulletin and the low turnover rate for paperboys, Edison began selling his own newspaper—the main reason being because he could make a lot more money per paper sold without having to pay overhead back to the newspaper publishers. Ingenious. And because he was working along the Grand Trunk Railroad, Edison had access to the news as it was coming to the town (communication revolved around the Railroad in those days as well). The paper was called the Grand Trunk Herald and turned into a huge hit with the passengers who were constantly boarding and getting off their trains. While this venture would prove successful, the success would not last long on the Railroads.

Edison was also a very curious child and was fascinated with the technology in and around the RailRoads. Due to his curiosity, Edison would soon begin conducting experiments. One day, one of his experiments went wrong (massive understatement), when he accidentally started a chemical fire inside the baggage car. Although the young man was essentially banned from working at that station ever again, an interest in science had been sparked.

> *"Opportunity is missed by most people because it is dressed in overalls and looks like work."*

Edison definitely worked hard. After working for years as a telegrapher, a career he began at the young age of 15, Edison created his first patent based on the technology he had been working on for so long, a voter recording machine. Although the invention didn't sell, Edison learned an important lesson in inventing: you sell your inventions when you solve problems. Because his machine didn't actually solve any problems for the legislators who voted, they were not interested.

Therefore, his next invention was a stock ticker that helped to speed up the process of stock market transactions. The invention was wildly successful with exchanges and brokers and helped to launch Edison's career. It wasn't long before Edison had his own lab in Newark, New Jersey, where he had high hopes of cranking out more groundbreaking inventions, which, of course, he did.

Telegraph and Communications

Edison decided to invent in the industry he knew best, the telegraph and communications industry. During the 19th century, people were looking for new ways to transmit messages and communicate more efficiently to keep up with the huge influx of industrialism sweeping the globe. When Alexander Graham Bell invented the Telephone Edison really felt the pressure to compete with the genius inventor. However, despite expanding his operations to other parts of New Jersey and hiring several machinists, Edison never could make anything as groundbreaking as Bell did. The closest he ever got was the first 2-way telegraph communication system, which, although not as important as the telephone was at the time, taught Edison a very important lesson about the inventing game.

Before Edison could get his invention selling at Railroad, a tycoon thieved his invention and only paid for it after Edison sued him in court. Edison received $100,000 and a lesson in how the market works in the late 1800s. The lesson being that ideas are only good if you own them and monetize them.

From then on, Edison invented and patented some of the most socioeconomically significant pieces of technology in human history. Here's a brief list of some of the more important ones. The most important one of all, arguably, is the phonograph. But it could easily be tied with the light bulb. Another invention is the motion picture camera, yes, the motion picture camera. In 1886 Thomas Edison was the first person to show a piece of cinema, thus launching one of the most influential art forms in modern history.

Despite the importance of the other two inventions, the majority of people associate the light bulb with Thomas Edison, as they always pair the discovery of electricity with Ben Franklin. The only problem with these correlations is that they are based on a big pile of lies. Neither Edison nor Franklin were actually the first to invent or discover either of those things. They merely improved upon work that came before them. Edison even said once:

"I start where the last man left off."

Rivalry with Tesla
Overall, however, Edison should be given credit for making the light bulb what it is today, along with cinema and the music industry, among many other things.

Through Edison's knack for economizing his inventions, he took the light bulb and quite literally lit up the world. The main catalyst that made his light bulb patent so effective and unique was how the currents worked. This brings us, finally, to the electrical currents master, Nikola Tesla, and one of the biggest industrialist rivalries of all time. Today it is Jeff Bezos and Elon Musk, but in the late 1800s and early 20th century, the top dogs were Thomas Edison and Nikola Tesla. Here are a few words they had for each other during their inventing and entrepreneurial careers:

> *"His [Thomas Edison] method was inefficient in the extreme, for an immense ground had to be covered to get anything at all unless blind chance intervened and, at first, I was almost a sorry witness of his doings, knowing that just a little theory and calculation would have saved him 90 percent of the labor. But he had a veritable contempt for book learning and mathematical knowledge, trusting himself entirely to his inventor's instinct and practical American sense. In view of this, the truly prodigious amount of his actual accomplishments is little short of a miracle."*

Edison and Tesla's beef could be condensed to two abbreviations: A/C and D/C. Although they disagreed on many things, electricity was the thing that drove them apart. Because believe it or not, Tesla actually got his start working for Edison. Tesla eventually left, however, due to him wanting to use exclusively A/C power instead of trying to convert it to D/C as Edison wanted. The move was classic Edison, in that it converting A/C to D/C was much easier to sell to consumers than the more erratic A/C. Edison electrocuted stray dogs, cats, and even a circus elephant just to prove how dangerous A/C was in public displays!

The rivalry between the two serves as a perfect microcosm for Thomas Edison's business and inventing philosophy, which can be summarized as: Take an old invention and make a sellable/scalable revision. That is the legacy Edison leaves behind, a changed world that would perhaps not look remotely the same without him.

Overall, Edison offers up many important lessons. However, there is one that protrudes further out than all the others. And it's something he and Tesla can both agree on. In Edison's own words he said:

"Genius is one percent inspiration and ninety-nine percent perspiration."

In other words, hard work, hard work, hard work, and then a little inspiration. Take it from him, arguably the most successful inventor of all time, that hard work can take you pretty far in life and might even make you a genius.

CHAPTER 2

Sigmund Freud

(1856 – 1939)

Austrian Neurologist / Founder of Psychoanalysis

"Look into the depths of your own soul and learn first to know yourself, then you will understand why this illness was bound to come upon you and perhaps you will thenceforth avoid falling ill."

- *Sigmund Freud*

Have you ever been psychoanalyzed by that annoying friend who never smiles and says "well actually," a lot? Or maybe you are that friend, in which case you have the legendary psychologist Sigmund Freud to thank for the gift of psychoanalysis and many other founding principles of psychology.

Early Life and College

Born in 1856, Freud grew up in a world where the pseudo-science of psychology was relatively new. In his career, Freud would revolutionize the field, discovering many different theories and insights into everything from dreams to parental trauma. Though many of his ideas and said discoveries have been disputed and discredited since, Freud nevertheless helped shape psychology into what it is today. So prepare yourself for the life of Sigmund Freud. And to hear the words libido and sexuality a few more times than you probably otherwise thought you would.

Freud was born in the Austrian Empire. A nation that would one day be annexed into Nazi Germany and in turn, pose a great danger to Sigmund Freud. Simply because the legendary psychologist so happened to be Jewish. When Freud began attending the University of Vienna, he initially wanted to study law. Fortunately for the future of psychoanalysis, Freud was pulled into the sciences. Though he started out in the biological field of zoology, Freud ended up getting a Master's Degree and going into the medical field.

One of his professors at the University, the zoology

professor, in fact, happened to be a Darwinist. This evolutionary-laced education would lead Freud to adopt a 'survival of the fittest approach to psychology, which some scholars believe he took a little too far at times.

Freud's first theoretical work was actually on the popular stimulant cocaine, a drug that Freud advocated all his professional career for its perceived health benefits (yes, health benefits). The paper Freud wrote on what 19th-century folks called 'coca', was successful and led to the budding medical professional being hired as a university lecturer in 1885.

Move towards Psychology

From there, Freud's career began turning more and more towards the study of the human mind. Back in his hospital working days, Freud spent time in the local asylum and a nearby psychiatric clinic, where Freud was personally exposed to the darker side of the brain. Biographers believe that this physical exposure to the behavior of mentally sick people intrigued Freud enough to continue with his studying of the mind that starting with examining the positive side effects of cocaine use.

In an odd leap of psychological subjects, Freud began studying the practice of hypnosis, which he eventually took up himself as a treatment for his patients. Freud started his hypnosis practice in Vienna in 1886 after learning about the technique during a study in Paris. However, Freud soon abandoned the practice due to its lack of clinical inconsistencies. Some patients improved drastically, while others did not. Freud found another method far more effective—a type of listening that encouraged a safe and accepting environment in which to speak, an environment where people could freely verbalize their complicated thoughts. If this method sounds like therapy, it wasn't exactly. At least not the therapy we know today. What Freud was moving toward was what he called psychoanalysis. At the time, this method of psychological treatment was brand new. This, in turn, later developed into modern-day therapy.

Although Catholic confessions had been a form of therapy, the priests involved usually offered forgiveness instead of advice or a pseudo-scientific analysis of one's problems. The dozens of revolutionary (and strange) theories Freud came up with from his many analyses of his patients became the cornerstone of his legacy on western culture, science, and the onset of treatments based on the methods of psychoanalysis.

I have to briefly mention the unhealthy practice Freud attributed to his great career success, and no, I'm not talking about coca. From the age of 24, Freud credited his ability to theorize so effectively to the nicotine found in tobacco. Smoking certainly helped him develop upper respiratory problems, as well as providing Freud's brain with a shot of happy chemicals throughout the day. In 1938, after escaping Nazi-controlled Austria, those happy little chemicals killed Freud via cancer of the jaw.

Another interesting fact about Freud is that despite

being an exceptionally awesome clinical psychologist, he still dreamed of being a prestigious university professor. Emphasis on prestigious. In 1902 he received the title of 'professor extraordinarius' despite not having any academic duties or university employment, with the exception of being a regular lecturer at the university's psychiatric clinic.

The title was more of an honorary degree than an actual earned title—a way for the university to put their name on a well-known psychologist and vice versa. When Freud became professor extraordinarius, he earned himself a high level of academic prestige. However, this prestige was earned through bribery, not because the University of Vienna was absolutely in love with Freud's theories.

IPA and Relationship with Yung

Like his predecessor Nietzche, Freud published ideas that were as controversial then as they are today. In order to grow his ideas into the roots of the psychological community, Freud founded an organization called the IPA (no , not like the beer) to promote and teach his theories on psychoanalysis. IPA stands for International Association of Psychoanalysts, which doesn't exactly fit the acronym but try not to think about that, grammar police. The IPA was founded in 1910, over a decade since Freud invented psychoanalysis. Freud had several followers, including a now-famous man named Carl Jung (see series 2). Freud was like a father figure to Jung in the beginning, and the two would talk in-depth for hours about deep psychology topics such as dreams and the subconscious. They would sit and debate their opinions, both happy to have finally found someone that thinks on their level. Eventually, however, they would part ways due to strong differing opinions and no shortage of stubbornness. Along with that, in just a few years after the IPA's founding, Freud's other bright young followers proved to be a little too bright and split, also going off to do their own studies and formulate their own theories that often differed from Freud's.

Many of Sigmund's ideas have never been universally accepted. The majority of his theories centered on the person's upbringing and repressed sexuality, making many of his published works taboo in the hyper-conservative turn-of-the-century sexual attitude. To a society that didn't like talking publicly about sex, Freud blaming all our problems on sex was a wild idea.

Nevertheless, here are some explanations of the main concepts and theories he developed that were of most significance to the world of psychology.

Id, Ego, and Superego
According to Freud, These are the three essential parts of the human personality. The id can be described as the impulsive, primitive, and irrational unconscious that operates solely on the outcome of pleasure or pain and is responsible for instincts related to both sex and aggression. The ego is the "I" people perceive that

evaluates the outside physical and social world and makes plans and decisions accordingly. And finally, the superego is the moral voice and conscience that attempts to guide the ego. And violating it will result in feelings of guilt and anxiety. Freud believed the superego was mostly formed within the first five years of life based on the moral standards and actions of a person's parents, and it continued to be influenced into adolescence by other role models.

Psychic Energy

Freud presupposes that the id was the basic source of psychic energy or the force that drives all mental processes. In particular, he believed that libido, or sexual urges, was a psychic energy that drives all human actions, and the libido is countered by Thanatos, which is the death instinct that drives all forms of destructive behavior.

Oedipus Complex

Between the ages of three and five, Freud proposed that as a normal part of their development process, all kids are sexually attracted to the parent of the opposite sex and in competition with the parent of the same sex. The theory is named after the Greek legend of Oedipus, who killed his father so he could marry his mother. A controversial theory that many don't agree on.

Dream Analysis

In his book, which probably contains his most prolific

work, *The Interpretation of Dreams*, Freud believed that people dreamed for a reason, such as to cope with real-life problems and situations that the mind is struggling with subconsciously and can't deal with consciously. This is his most thought-provoking and relative theory in today's world and has since long been debated and further analyzed. Freud believed that dreams were fueled by a person's wishes and desires. He also believed that by analyzing our dreams and memories, we can begin to understand them, which can subconsciously influence our current behavior and feelings when we are awake. He believed there were common themes that occurred in dreams universally.

We've all heard of the dream, or nightmare I should say, of having your teeth fall out, which can be interpreted as having stress or anxiety in your life, or a loss of a relationship or even a relative. The whole concept has been deeply theorized and researched ever since.

Legacy

Not all of his ideas hold much water nowadays. Especially since we now have much more plausible theories about female sexuality. However, Freud's ideas are seen more as concepts that were filled out later versus well-thought-out theories. A literary critic sums it up quite eloquently when she says: *"Freud has no rivals among his successors because they think he wrote science, when in fact he wrote art."*

But is that Freud's legacy? Just concepts? As previously mentioned, after the IPA fallout, the defectors left and started their own schools based on psychoanalysis. Carl Jung and Jungian psychology is by far the most notable, with popular psychologist Jordan Peterson often referring back to Jung in his own theories and lectures today. Although they all changed the recipe a bit, each school's philosophy was built on Freud's overall concept. These psychologists unknowingly spread the idea around the world like missionaries preaching the gospel, ensuring that Freud's teachings would leave a permanent mark in the field of psychology. Modern therapy is based on the concept of psychoanalysis, which is merely a psychiatrist participating in a conversation with a patient to treat psychopathology. Freud summarizes the benefits of his invention by saying,

> *"Unexpressed emotions will never die. They are buried alive and will come forth later in uglier ways."*

Meaning that you should avoid becoming an emotional volcano and go see a therapist, who might not exist if not for Freud deciding that hypnosis was a waste of time. And if he had been afraid to share his often bizarre ideas with a world that usually opposes the weird and strange, we may not have made such strides in the field since. Here are some final thought-provoking words from the great mind:

"Where does a thought go when it's forgotten?"

"The madman is a dreamer awake"
"One day, in retrospect, the years of struggle will strike you as the most beautiful."

"Out of your vulnerabilities will come your strength."

CHAPTER 3

Julius Caesar
(100BC – 44BC)

Ancient Roman Emperor

"I came to Rome when it was a city of stone ... and left it a city of marble"

\-   *Julius Caesar*

In 75 BCE, a 25-year-old Gaius Julius Caesar was captured by civilian pirates and held for ransom. Caesar had initially been on an innocent trip to study oratory at Rhodes when he was captured; sailing with a fleet that indicated his high status led to the pirates seeing and taking a silver opportunity. It was silver because the pirates demanded 20 silver talents, the modern equivalent of around $28 million, which was eventually paid to the pirates in full.

When Caesar was released, he did not go back home and cry on his mom's shoulder, nor did he take a vacation to recuperate his emotional health. Instead, Julius Caesar quickly gathered a fleet of his, which was well within his power as a Roman nobleman, and sailed out after the pirates. Caesar found them, captured them, and had all of them crucified.

Most people, even history buffs, are unfamiliar with that story but not in the least surprised by its content. From the pizza chain restaurant Little Caesars to the many adaptations of the William Shakespeare play, our culture has been fed the image of Julius Caesar, the ancient conqueror. And tales of crucifying pirates only add to that legend. But Caesar's life was more than just conquering foreign lands for Rome. It was full of drama and tragic romance, betrayal (I'm looking at you, Brutus), and a decision that changed the course of world history.

Early Life
Caesar's life began in 100 BCE in Italy, where he was

brought into the affluent Caesar family, who did not become politically active until Julius's father became the governor of Rome's Asian territories. Apparently, Julius inherited his father's political ambitions because, from an early age, Caesar was preparing for a career serving Rome. The primary and most effective method Caesar used to serve his republic was through military means. In fact, many historians consider Caesar one of the most successful military leaders in all of history. Time and time again, he defeated foreign adversaries as well as his fellow Roman generals in battle. And for Caesar, that legendary career began at a young age. When he was just 16, Julius's father died suddenly, leaving him the head of his family, which was much more significant than you might think. Caesar's family could trace their roots back to the original noble families of Rome during the early days of the city's founding. This high level of familial legacy was now thrust upon the shoulders of teenage Julius Caesar, including the future of the family's political aspirations, which had been lackadaisical over the past couple of centuries, considering their high-born lineage.

In addition to inheriting a fractured family legacy, Caesar, upon becoming the head of his family, was given a civil war between his uncle Gaius Marius and his nemesis Lucius Cornelius Sulla. The rivalry took Roman politics by storm, and though he was not directly involved in his uncle's conflict, Caesar's life was greatly affected by the war.

When his uncle lost against Sully, Caesar had

recently been promoted to the high priest of Jupiter and married Cornelia, the daughter of Cinna, a close war ally to his uncle Gaius Marius. All of these accomplishments were terminated when Sulla's regime took over Rome. Caesar's inheritance was confiscated along with his newly acquired position and dowry. However, when he was ordered to divorce his wife Cornelia, Caesar refused to do so and went into hiding until his mother's side of the family helped to smooth things over with Sulla. Nevertheless, Sulla still disliked Caesar, reportedly saying that the young man had some of his Uncle Gaius in him. And Caesar, still wary of Sulla, decided the best thing to do would be to join the army. This cautious decision was what first brought Caesar into his now world-famous military career.

Military

Caesar began by serving under two generals and earned great reviews for his service. But when he heard that Sulla had died, Caesar returned to Rome at last, finding a modest house in the middle-class area of the city to live in for the time being due to his lost inheritance. The home purchase, however, proved to be an accidentally genius move by Caesar. After moving back to Rome, he began a new career as a legal advocate. And in the process, won the hearts and minds of the low and middle-class citizens of Rome. Put another way, Caesar became the people's champion. As previously mentioned, Caesar had been captured by pirates on the way to learn oratory, a skill he was extremely gifted in throughout his life. Being a military genius helped him win battles, but his oratory talents helped him become Consul.

In case you don't know what a consul is, the consulship of Rome was the highest office one can hold in the republic. What made it distinct from, say, the American presidency or the Prime Minister of Britain was that there were two consuls, each serving to balance each other out power-wise. The Romans were initially protective of their constitution, which was founded on no one man ruling Rome at any one time. And when Caesar was elected consul, he would be one of the last, adhering to a principle he lived and literally died by:

"If you must break the law, do it to seize power: in all other cases observe it."

Caesar's consulship kicked off with the first order of business, marrying off his daughter to a politician named Pompey to obtain a peace agreement between the three most powerful men in Rome. The three rulers included Caesar himself, Pompey, and the latter's rival Crassus.

Caesar's second order of business was to redistribute land to the poor, a move that angered the aristocratic senate, who would be opposed to Caesar's plebeian-focused politics until they had had enough (we'll get to that part in a few paragraphs). The redistribution was also supported by the other two members of the three rulers, Pompey and Crassus.

Between those three, the policies were enforced with spears and swords in case the senate decided to "manually" oppose the new legislation. When his consulship ended, Caesar feared that he would be prosecuted for the politically aggressive acts he committed while in power and swiftly returned back to the province he governed.

However, Caesar had far more than angry aristocratic senators to worry about. During his consulship campaign, Caesar had borrowed significant amounts of money and now found himself out of office, with debtors to pay off. In Caesar's day, there were a couple of ways Roman governors could make some quick cash. One method was to extort their subjects and citizens. The second method was war. Just as they still do in modern times, ancient governments would take spoils from war and keep them for themselves. In Caesar's case, if he went out and conquered a new territory or two, he could collect enough assets to pay off his debts. And Caesar, being a man of the people, decided war was the better option.

During Caesar's time in power, the primary foe of the republic were the Gauls, a group of indigenous tribes living in modern-day France. And it worked out quite nicely that Caesar's provinces bordered right along with the unconquered territories of Gaul, so the opportunity to get some equity back was ripe for the taking. During this period of his life, Caesar was already well-loved by the people, but the Gallic Wars would make him into a legend.

Summarizing the war in a simple and very famous sentence, Caesar wrote:

"I came, I saw, I conquered."

To pay off his debt and increase his power, Caesar had to win. And Gaul was a formidable place. There was a reason Rome had not conquered them yet. The Gauls and other tribes of central Europe were remote and tough to defeat.

Caesar took four legions with him on his campaign into the unstable (by Roman standards) and hostile tribal land of Gaul. His victories were swift; the Gallic tribes were not united, and Caesar was easily able to exploit that tribal division in battle, leading to Caesar conquering territories all the way up the southern shore of the English Channel, thus, giving the governor an open pass to conquer Britain. Rome had desired a path to Britain for some time, and now Caesar had literally paved the way for the legions of Rome to reach the island. When Caesar arrived in Britain, he saw, and he conquered the tribes there as well, solidifying his reputation as the most powerful man in Rome and perhaps the world. In subsequent centuries, the name Caesar would be synonymous with the title of emperor. Therefore, the title of Roman emperor was named after Caesar, the equivalent of the American presidency being named the 'Washington' of the United States. In other words, Rome was proud of their Caesar. Well, not all Romans.

Upon returning to Rome, Caesar was met with adulation and resentment from the politicians of the city. Namely the aristocrats who felt that Caesar was getting too powerful, and Pompey, who had broken off his alliance with Caesar and Crassus. Rome now expected civil war, similar to the battles fought between Caesar's uncle and Sulla only a couple of decades earlier. What was dubbed the First Triumvirate was now fragmented, with one broken piece being far superior in the skill of war strategy. The same man who brutally executed the pirates who captured him was now fighting for supremacy of Rome against his next pirate fleet, Pompey, who represented the Senate in a failed effort to control Caesar. But Caesar made easy work of Pompey, chasing him to Egypt, where he was brought the senate leader's severed head as a trophy for his victory.

Even before his victory in the civil war, Rome had elected Caesar's dictatorial powers. And he maintained them, or at least a consulship, until 45 BCE when he was elected as consul without a second compatriot serving beside him. By this point, Caesar had essentially been ruling Rome like a king for the past three years. After he finished off Pompey's sons, there was no one left to oppose Caesar outside of his family members and allies, such as Mark Antony and his grandnephew and handpicked heir, Octavian. And despite Caesar being about as aristocratic as a Roman could get, some of the old families running the senate still despised his autocratic rule. Caesar once said:

"I am prepared to resort to anything, to submit to anything, for the sake of the commonwealth."

That included rewriting the republic constitution and centralizing the Roman government to achieve stability for the republic, which conflicted with the special interests of the aristocrats, who did not want a dictator rearranging their system.

Caesar and Cleopatra

Caesar became involved in an Egyptian civil war between the child pharaoh and his sister, wife, and co-regent queen, Cleopatra. As a result of the pharaoh's role in Pompey's murder, Caesar sided with Cleopatra. He survived the Siege of Alexandria, and later, he defeated the pharaoh's forces at the Battle of the Nile in 47 BC and installed Cleopatra as ruler. Caesar and Cleopatra celebrated their victory with a triumphal procession on the Nile in the spring of 47 BC. The royal barge was accompanied by 400 additional ships, and Caesar was introduced to the lavish lifestyle of the Egyptian pharaohs.

Caesar and Cleopatra did not marry. Caesar continued his relationship with Cleopatra throughout his last marriage. This did not constitute adultery in Roman eyes. He fathered a son called Caesarion. Cleopatra visited Rome on more than one occasion, residing in Caesar's villa just outside Rome across the Tiber. This was a mutually beneficial relationship. Cleopatra required the might of Caesar's armies to install her as ruler of Egypt, while Caesar required Cleopatra's vast wealth. She is believed to have been the world's richest woman at the time and able to finance Caesar's return to power in Rome.

Assassination

Though Caesar had overcome much adversity in his life, he could not stop his own assassination. On the Ides of March in 44 BCE, on March 15th, a group of Senators sprung on Caesar as he was entering the senate meeting, stabbing him an alleged 23 times before they decided to stop. The senators had finally exerted their long-held frustrations with Caesar, primarily in the name of the Roman version of democracy. Ironically, that was not how the people saw it. When word got out to the plebeians and other officials, they were outraged. Their anger helped stoke the flames of another civil war, stoked by the power vacuum left behind by Caesar.

The Roman dictator and political reformer had to overcome many difficulties in his life. He was forced to lead his family at 16, captured by pirates, and faced dozens of political foes, beating them all until the end.

"I had rather be first in a village than second at Rome."

"Divide and Conquer."

CHAPTER 4

Jesus Christ
(4BC – 30/33 AD)

Central Figure of Christianity

"I am the Way, the Truth, and the Life. No one comes to the Father except through me."

- *Jesus Christ*

Born sometime around 4 BCE and 1 AD, Yeshua, now known as Jesus, began his ministry preaching in the lands of Judea, announcing several controversial claims that produced a variety of reactions from Judeans. Among these claims are six words that would spark a movement by early Christianity and spread to every nook and cranny of the earth:

"I am the Son of God."

But who was this self-proclaimed Son of God? Well, in all honesty, we don't really know. Trying to paint an accurate historical portrait of Jesus Christ is like trying to get an unbiased opinion on the current US president. Christians believe him to be the divine savior of the world, Jews view him as just another phony Messiah executed by the Romans, while some historians doubt he even existed. The reason for this historical ambiguity is due to the lack of non-religious sources documenting Jesus' life. Most scholars, however, rely heavily on those religious sources for information. Primarily because they are biographies. Though their content is focused on Jesus's ministry, they do offer some details on aspects of Jesus' life, including his birth, which is now celebrated worldwide as Christmas.

It all begins when Mary, his mother, was visited by an angel of the Lord, who told the teenage Mary she would give birth to a child named Jesus and that he would be the Son of God. Unfortunately, the Angel had terrible timing because Mary was set to be married to a man named Joseph, which meant, under 1st-century Judean marital customs, she was supposed to be a virgin. Due to these complications, Mary and Joseph had some discussions before deciding to go through with their marriage—a brave proposition for Joseph, given the extremely rigid stigmas around pre-marital affairs often found in ancient Judea. And so Jesus was born of a virgin.

From there, the story explains how the odd couple arrived at the inn, Mary in labor, and were forced to deliver their literally God-given child inside a stable amongst livestock and some shepherds. That, according to the Gospel of Luke, is the story of how Jesus was born.

In fact, the only Gospel where this event takes place is in Luke, a book that ambitiously tries to push the narrative of a divine Jesus. Historians date the Gospel of Luke to around 80 AD to 110 AD, 50 to 80 years after Jesus was crucified by the Romans in 33 AD. The events leading up to this brutal execution are what make up the majority of what we know about Jesus's life. Starting in the first Gospel, Mark, we mainly get a series of sermons and a basic outline of Jesus's ministry. Within those sermons and stories, we get a potential hint as to who Jesus was as a person. In Mark verses 42-45, Jesus teaches a selfless way of living that is a central facet of Christianity:

"Whoever wants to be a leader among you must be your servant, and whoever wants to be first among you must be the slave of everyone else. For even the Son of Man came not to be served but to serve others and to give his life as a ransom for many."

Selflessness was a major aspect of Jesus's teachings to his disciples. One that carried over to Paul, who implemented into his letters that eventually became the official doctrines of Christianity.

The Man Nobody Knows

Before we dive into the gospels, I should mention an extraordinary piece of work called 'the man nobody knows' written by Bruce Barton in 1925. This book is a compelling portrait of Jesus, emphasizing the sometimes forgotten side of his character. It presents an unorthodox view of Christ as a buoyant, laughing, and virile man, a man of muscle, intellect, and recognizable emotions, and a profound high-spirited leader among men. Although controversial, it is worth a read. The author notes that books and books are written about Jesus as the son of God, but that his favorite title for himself was actually *'The son of Man.'*

The book speaks of the normal working-class life he lived up to the age of 30. Somewhere in those years, the consciousness of his divinity came to him. In the beginning, there were still many doubts, and those doubts lasted 40 days and 40 nights when Jesus did not eat and questioned everything. In this lonely struggle, he questioned whether he had made a mistake by leaving his good carpentry trade to become a wandering preacher. He was tempted by Satan many times, offering food and prosperity if he went back to his old life. At the end of the 40 days in the calm of that wilderness came the 'majestic conviction, which is the very soul of leadership. He never doubted himself or his mission from that point on. He spoke with such an aura and a certainty that he drew crowds everywhere he went. My favorite passage of this book is as follows:

> *-We speak of personal magnetism (of Jesus) as though there were something mysterious about it- a magic quality bestowed on one in a thousand and denied to the rest. This is not true. The essential element in personal magnetism is a consuming sincerity- an overwhelming faith in the importance of the work one has to do. Emerson said:*
>
> **"what you are thunders so loud I cannot hear what you say'**
>
> *The hardened french captain, Robert de Baudicourt, could hardly be expected to believe a peasant girl's story about heavenly voices promising she would do what the Dauphin armies couldn't. Yet he gave Joan of Arc her first sword.-*

Delving back into the Gospels, we catch a glimpse at who Jesus was, or at least who his subsequent followers thought he was or what they wanted him to be. Of course, we will be primarily focusing on the four Canonical Gospels. Not because they are the best or most interesting, but due to when they were written. Their dating ranges from around 60 AD all the way up to 200 AD. Most historians believe these to be the best source we have, especially the Gospel of Mark, the reason that the estimated time frame begins with 60 AD. Dates are usually the boring part of history, and I hope that you'll forgive me for using so many. But they, along with the Gospels themselves, help us shed light on Jesus. The four canonical Gospels (Mark, Matthew, Luke, and John) are filled with Jesus preaching to his followers and local audiences, dissing Pharisees, and even bringing people back from the dead. Aside from his miracles, Jesus is most famous for his many parables. Many scholars credit Jesus's parables with setting a moral precedence for western society. Stories such as the familiar *"Good Samaritan"* and the *"Prodigal Son"* have been passed down through generations through millions of church sermons, art, and Sunday School lessons. The Good Samaritan, being the more well-known, goes:

> *"A man was going down from Jerusalem to Jericho, when he was attacked by robbers. They stripped him of his clothes, beat him and went away, leaving him half dead. A priest happened to be going down the same road, and when he saw the man, he passed by on the other side. So too, a Levite, when he came to the place and saw him, passed by on the other side. But a Samaritan, as he*

traveled, came where the man was; and when he saw him, he took pity on him. He went to him and bandaged his wounds, pouring on oil and wine. Then he put the man on his own donkey, brought him to an inn and took care of him. The next day he took out two denarii and gave them to the innkeeper. 'Look after him,' he said, 'and when I return, I will reimburse you for any extra expense you may have.'

The Good Samaritan has been a tale of compassion, understanding, and open-mindedness that translates to people even today. Back in ancient Roman-controlled Judea, the parable served as a story of peace in a time of political angst fueled by resentment towards anyone who the Jews considered to be gentile, which happened to be everyone who was not Jewish. Jesus was trying to reach his people by telling them stories to help them see his vision for a new Judea and for Christians, a vision for the whole world. Some of his teachings even defy the basic instincts of humanity. Verses like Matthew 5:44, which instructs you to,

> **"Love your enemies and pray for those who persecute you, so that you may be sons of your Father who is in heaven; for he makes his sun rise on the evil and on the good, and sends rain on the just and on the unjust."**

And Matthew 19:23-24 where Jesus says:

"I tell you the truth, it is hard for a rich man to enter the kingdom of heaven. Again I tell you, it is easier for a camel to go through the eye of a needle than for a rich man to enter the kingdom of heaven."

Both verses show Jesus' mindset and how he wished the world to be. Of course, these teachings go against how many people choose to live their life, which is for themselves. Though these concepts were not new, they did, according to the gospels, cause the religious leaders of the day, the 'dissed out of their robes' Pharisees, to resent Jesus. The gospels portray them as the ones who had Jesus crucified. However, according to historians, it is more likely that Jesus was executed by the Romans for being a perceived rabble-rouser, even though Jesus supposedly claimed his revolution was of the soul and not the political.

Death

His brutal death, which any reasonable historian will agree did occur, is by far the most famous moment in history. Crucifixions were a common form of publicly killing defectors and criminals in the Roman Empire. But as Jesus was suffering on the cross, he was making a sacrifice for a religion and its people and, in the process, creating one of the most well-known iconographies on earth.

Today it is estimated there are around 2 billion

Christians worshiping in 2021. For many of those people, the image of Jesus' sacrifice means a great deal to them. Through his death, Jesus has given many of his followers, known as Christians, comfort and guidance in their lives. His story alone is incredible. Going from a couple of thousand followers to 2 billion is not a typical 'rags to riches' story like you will find in the rest of this book—it's a story of minds.

From the verse Mathew 5:40 the bible says:

> *'As for the one who wants to sue you and take away your shirt, let him have your coat as well.'*

This is such a powerful teaching. In today's world, we often get so caught up in our materialistic possessions. Imagine how a thief would feel if he stole $10 from your pocket and you then offered him another $10. To show that level of compassion at that moment for a troubled man who is clearly on the wrong path in life could be life-changing. Could you be the bigger person in certain scenarios in your life? In the words of Jesus himself:

> *"It is more blessed to give than to receive" (Acts 20:35)*

Because no one has been able to captivate and rule as many minds as Jesus Christ. Take his story and many teachings as an inspiration for your life. Whether or not you choose to believe in him as a deity that people see in the clouds, or just a spiritual leader like Buddha, you can still examine his life and retain a simple message: That your words and actions can be powerful and touch people's souls for millennia to come—as a savior of the world, a revolutionary, a teacher. Regardless of what you want to call him, Jesus Christ is one of the most influential people to have ever lived.

CHAPTER 5

Sir John Franklin
(1786 – 1847)

Arctic Explorer

"God worked in their lives in proportion to the degree of the koinonia, the quality of love between believers. Their favor with God flowed largely from his pleasure of their depth of fellowship."

- John Franklin, And the Place Was Shaken: How to Lead a Powerful Prayer Meeting

Sir John Franklin, also known as the "man who ate his own boots," was one of the most accomplished and controversial explorers in history. He received the long nickname of the man who ate his boots after one of his first expeditions, the infamous Coppermine expedition, which he was picked to lead in 1819. The expedition had some food shortages, allegedly forcing Franklin to eat the leather from his pair of boots. Despite the humiliation, John Franklin was probably glad to be there. His climb to that high position was not an easy one, which included having to climb the social ladder. As the chapter name indicates, Sir John Franklin eventually became knighted for his accomplishments, being one of the few members of his family to make a name for himself.

Early Life
From the moment he was born in 1786 in Lincolnshire, England, Franklin had a chip on his shoulder. That was the mindset any Englishman, or even an Englishwoman, had to possess to climb up the social hierarchy. If you've ever read or seen works of fiction such as Pride and Prejudice or Downton Abbey, you'll understand how important class jumping was for the Brits. In Franklin's case, his father was a merchant who could trace his ancestry from a long line of small landholding country gentlemen. That doesn't sound too bad. However, Franklin's mother was born into a family of farmers, making his lineage slightly asymmetrical in favor of being middle class.

He ended up being number 9 out of 12 children, which gave Franklin a close-up view of how his older siblings struggled to make a name for themselves in the fast-paced competitive Victorian economy. There were, however, a couple of his siblings who succeeded. One of his brothers ended up becoming a judge while another was employed by the East India Trading Company. Seeing the contrasts in socio-economic success found amongst his siblings placed a chip on Franklin's shoulder from an early age. He knew that he had to become successful at something lest he be a burden to his family. In fact, Franklin's father, in an effort to establish his son a stable, steady income, like many parents do, desired for his son to either go into the church or enter into business. But Franklin, by contrast, saw another path that would lead him to prosperity, the sea. After Franklin attended King Edward VI Grammar School, he decided he wanted to sail the seas, one way or another. Though his father was initially opposed to the idea, Franklin was able to convince him otherwise. Franklin was only 12 years old.

First Voyages
Franklin's first voyages at that young age were on merchant ships until his father used his influence to obtain a spot on the Royal Naval vessel HMS Polyphemus once he came of age. From there, Franklin had a very eventful Naval career. He ended up either participating in or witnessing some of the most important sea battles of the early 19th century. Franklin

was there for the Battle of Trafalgar and participated in the Battle of Pulo Aura. During the Battle of Lake Borgne, Franklin was wounded serving the Crown when it fought the newly created United States in the War of 1821. But it was the assistance he gave to Captain David Buchan on an expedition through the arctic waters of Norway that started Franklin on his journey towards becoming an arctic explorer. Franklin commanded his own ship of the HMS, and after he gained that rare experience from the icy voyage, the Royal Navy chose Franklin to lead the Coppermine expedition.

First Major Expedition and Controversy
The goal that the Navy wanted to reach on the Coppermine expedition was to chart the land from Hudson Bay to the Northern coast of Canada. Much of the far North, including many parts of Canada, had yet to be explored by Europeans. With that inherent curiosity, and a need to chart their never-ending territory of Canada, Franklin set out on his first expedition, perhaps not realizing what a hellish experience it would be.

Coppermine was a complete shit show by modern standards. The entire expedition lasted three years, from 1819 to 1822. Only 9 of the original 20 men that embarked alongside Franklin returned back to their homes at the end of the expedition, and the circumstances under which they died are still under scrutiny today by historians. Of course, the majority of his men died from more natural causes. Some died from exhaustion due to the sheer workload and lack of nourishment. Others were said to have succumbed to starvation. The few that managed to find some food were not exactly eating from a 5-star restaurant. In order to survive, the nine men who made it were forced to eat lichen from the rocks and trees around them, and then there was Franklin, who ate his boots. But some scholars believe that Franklin and his crew could not have survived that long on lichen and leather alone. Some speculate that the crew resorted to cannibalism. The vast majority of scholars agree that there was murder, which was probably carried out not due to a violent disagreement but for survival purposes.

According to the journals of the men who survived, one man named Terohaute was responsible for what happened. A company of 4 men, of which Terohaute was a part of, were supposed to return to their camp from Franklin's camp 4 miles away, and only Terohaute came back. Terohaute claimed that he had been separated from the other three, but was fortunate enough to have killed a hare and a partridge. Any sort of worry or suspicion was thrown aside in favor of enjoying the fresh fowl that Terohaute had brought them. Then, just two days later, Terohaute returned with more meat, claiming he had taken it off a wolf he had killed. The men enjoyed this seemingly miraculous source of sustenance. They, however, did not enjoy it when Terohaute began acting erratic and mysterious. On many occasions, he would disappear for long periods of time and then, when asked where he's been, refuse to give the other three men any information. It was at this point that the other men became suspicious of Terohaute, believing that he had murdered his three fellow explorers and was living off their flesh and sharing it with them in the form of "hare" and "wolf" meat. In the journals, however, they never find any evidence to support these theories.

Later on, they do describe the death of their companion named Robert Hood. After hearing a gunshot in the woods, the two other men, John Richardson and John Hepburn searched the area. They found Hood dead from a bullet to the head and Terohaute walking carrying a firearm. Terohaute claimed that Hood had been killed from an accidental headshot (from his own weapon). However, his rifle was too long for him to reach the trigger while holding the barrel to his head. Richardson and Hepburn knew the story was bogus. But with themselves now on Terohaute's chopping block (literally), they needed to do something quickly. So, one day when Terohaute had gone out to gather up some lichen, Richardson loaded up his handgun and waited until Terohaute got back to camp before shooting him dead, ending the violence at last.

The claims of murder were only ever written down by the explorers, so there is no evidential proof that any of it ever happened. However, we know for certain that only nine men returned. And when they did, the reception from the Royal Navy was not positive. The expedition had cost much human life, with very little charting to show for it. Many of Franklin's peers questioned his competence, many citing the poor planning and mismanagement of the crew as evidence. Franklin's superior, the man who had ordered the expedition in the first place, wrote the most scathing review of all:

> *"[He] has not the physical powers required for the labor of moderate Voyaging in this country; he must have three meals per diem, Tea is indispensable, and with the utmost exertion he cannot walk above Eight miles in one day, so that it does not follow if those Gentlemen are unsuccessful that the difficulties are insurmountable."*

The disastrous Coppermine expedition left Franklin in serious doubt of his future in the Navy, or in the British government for that matter. He certainly could have been thinking of his family and what they would think if he ultimately failed to recover from his social humiliation.

Fortunately, the Royal Navy allowed Franklin to lead the next expedition into the Canadian arctic. But on this occasion, they left the supply logistics up to the Hudson Bay Company, allowing Franklin to focus on the land-exploring aspect of the job. The expedition would end up being a success, with Franklin and his fellow explorer John Richardson leading them to chart lands never mapped by Europeans. On August 16th, 1825, Franklin became just the second European to reach the mouth of the Mackenzie River. For this accomplishment, Franklin became Sir John Franklin. King George IV knighted Franklin upon his return to England in 1829, making him the first member of his family to earn a title through accomplishment alone.

With his title and improved reputation, Franklin, aged 53, was made lieutenant governor of Van Diemen's Land, known today as the island of Tasmania. To this day, a statue of Franklin sits in the center of Franklin Square in his honor. Oddly enough, despite all the honors, Franklin only served six years as lieutenant governor before being removed from office.

1845 Expedition to find the Northwest Passage

Franklin will be best known for leading the tragic 1845 expedition to find the Northwest Passage. He and his crew were extremely close to discovering the elusive sea route through the Canadian North. This expedition, often called the Franklin Expedition, remains one of the most enduring mysteries of Arctic exploration and Canadian history.

He was asked to lead this arctic expedition despite being 59 years old. Of course, due to his age, Franklin was not their first pick, but he had more experience than most captains in the British military had when it came to arctic exploration. Being tasked with exploring the uncharted areas of the Northwest Passage was an exciting prospect and big news back home. But unfortunately, it would also be his last voyage.

Two years into the expedition and no one had received a letter from Franklin. His wife, Jane, more commonly known as Lady Franklin, began calling for a search party to be launched to find her husband. When they finally did begin searching, all they found were ships and bones. Scholars and explorers are still not sure if they have recovered the body of Franklin. They do suspect that the expedition went disastrously bad, with one man showing signs that his flesh was carved off his body after he died. However, scholars are certain that Franklin met his end traversing the Northwest Passage.

Franklin will go down as one of the great explorers in history, inspiring and paving the way for Roald Amundsen some 50 years later, who became the first explorer to navigate the Northwest Passage by ship, the original goal of the Franklin expedition, in 1903-1906.

Franklin loved the sea and never turned down the chance to explore the extremely dangerous arctic. Despite the tragic ending, if you take anything away from the life of Franklin, let it be that you are going to have to learn to deal with failures in life, but never give up on your goal, and you too could etch yourself into history books.

CHAPTER 6

Sun Tzu

(544 BC - 496 BC)

Chinese General & Military Strategist
Writer of 'The Art of War

"Let your plans be dark and impenetrable as night, and when you move, fall like a thunderbolt."

- *Sun Tzu*

Can war be artful? According to Sun Tzu, war is just another art, another craft to be learned along with painting and cooking. In a post-Vietnam and Iraq war world, we often view war as a violently cruel concept, and not a philosophy that can be learned like stoicism or nihilism. Nevertheless, ancient Chinese military general and tactician Sun Tzu wrote one of the most famous books on philosophy and strategy of all time. **The Art of War** has influenced countless military leaders and thinkers over the 2,000-plus years of its existence. Of all those people, the vast majority of them, including you, the reader, would be surprised to discover that Sun Tzu most likely didn't exist as a historical figure, at least according to some historians.

The main issue with proving the historical existence of Sun Tzu is the evidence because there is almost zero to speak of. There are many historical people whose existence historians debate, including Jesus. However, the general and writer known as Sun Tzu, whoever he was, still left a big mark on the world. Even though in ancient China, Sun Tzu probably would have been known as Sun Wu, and most likely did not even write the book that is now widely attributed to his name. History can be confusing sometimes, and this is one of those times. The bottom line is that scholars have no clue who actually wrote the Art of War. Some historians even theorize that the military guide was pieced together by several different Chinese authors over the centuries, who each added their own bits of wisdom. There are many different theories and opinions of Sun Tzu, and none of them is a clear winner among scholars. This means this biography will be a little different from the others in this book.

The Art of War

The story that is traditionally told in the Art of War is not exactly a perfect source to draw an accurate picture of Sun Tzu, who either helped write the book or is the inspiration on which the Art of War is based. As the questionable legend goes, Sun Tzu was a brilliant military strategist who came from an aristocratic military family. He was born in 544 BCE and died in 496 BCE after a career as a general. Later records, such as the Spring and Autumn Annals, describe Sun Tzu as a legendary figure in China and attribute the Art of War's brilliance to his genius. And perhaps they are telling the truth. There very well could have been a Sun Tzu who wrote down his military methods and passed them down to other thinkers who revised and added to the book themselves over the years, morphing the book into what it is today. Or Sun Tzu could have been the mere inspiration for the Art of War. We will never know for sure. Many historians believe that he was a military figure during the Spring and Autumn period, though he may not have been as high-ranking as later legends would perpetuate. So the questions remain. Are we getting a glimpse into the mind of Sun Tzu, or is this a Chinese bible on the principles of war?

Regardless of the true answer, the book has taken on a life of its own. Very few ancient texts survive today, and even fewer are read by modern eyes as fervently as the Art of War. The real question is, what makes the Art of War so special? Ever since it was published in the 5th century, the Art of War has inspired everyone from Churchill to television gangsters. Tony Soprano, a mafia leader from the show The Sopranos, stated in an episode after reading the book:

> *"Here's this guy, a Chinese general, who wrote this thing 2400 years ago, and most of it still applies today!"*

Obviously, a screenwriter wrote that, but one did write this quote from a real military legend, known as American general George Douglas MacArthur, who once said:

> *"I always kept a copy of The Art of War on my desk."*

Imaginary gangsters and famous generals are good company to be in. Though they may be different people with very different moral and et   hical standards, they both have one thing in common, both men want to win, and reading the Art of War can help you do just that. There are several passages in the book that mention winning:

> **"To win one hundred victories in one hundred battles is not the acme of skill. To subdue the enemy without fighting is the acme of skill."**

Then this one:

> *"Thus we may know that there are five essentials for victory:*
>
> *1. He will win who knows when to fight and when not to fight.*
> *2. He will win who knows how to handle both superior and inferior forces.*
> *3. He will win whose army is animated by the same spirit throughout all its ranks.*
> *4. He will win who, prepared himself, waits to take the enemy unprepared.*
> *5. He will win who has military capacity and is not interfered with by the sovereign."*

How to achieve victory over your opponent. That is what the Art of War is about. Because that is primarily what the author who wrote it was concerned with at the time. The Art of War was written and inspired by a tumultuous period of time in ancient China, a time of war. The previously mentioned Spring and Autumn period was a brutal one for China. Many of the vassal states run by wealthy aristocrats fought each other ruthlessly for underpopulated and unclaimed land, leading the demand for cunning generals to skyrocket. Amongst these military men, Sun Tzu emerges and becomes the alleged author when it is published later on down the road.

It makes sense that a long warring period would mold someone like Sun Tzu. The rough times forced the military leaders of the day to think creatively in order to defeat their opponents. Hence quotes like:

> *"There are not more than five musical notes, yet the combinations of these five give rise to more melodies than can ever be heard.*
>
> *"There are not more than five primary colours, yet in combination they produce more hues than can ever been seen."*
>
> *"There are not more than five cardinal tastes, yet combinations of them yield more flavours than can ever be tasted."*

And:

> *"If your enemy is secure at all points, be prepared for him. If he is in superior strength, evade him. If your opponent is temperamental, seek to irritate him. Pretend to be weak, that he may grow arrogant. If he is taking his ease, give him no rest. If his forces are united, separate them. If sovereign and subject are in*

accord, put division between them. Attack him where he is unprepared, appear where you are not expected."

Put another way. You win the battles before you ever swing a sword or release an arrow. You win with the mindset you bring to the battle. This can be applied to all walks of life, not just war. Essentially what all this means, according to "Sun Tzu" is to be adaptive. And in order to be adaptive, you need to think creatively. Your enemy needs to be thrown off guard. In our modern times, there is a reason lawyers are some of the biggest fans of the Art of War. Even in something as technical as the study of law, creative strategizing is a major catalyst in your odds of beating another attorney. Tony Soprano wasn't joking around when he said that this book is versatile. It can even apply to someone managing cashiers at a McDonald's. Take this passage, for example:

"Treat your men as you would your own beloved sons. And they will follow you into the deepest valley."

This nugget of wisdom can apply to anyone who manages people. If you've ever worked at a job before, you'll understand the difference between a good manager and one you curse at in your head every time you walk by them. Because it's a strong contrast, believe me.

The Art of War is much more than just a book on war. It is a book on how to be a better person. In fact, it gives some advice that you may not expect from a war guide. As this famous quote indicates:

> *"If you know the enemy and know yourself, your victory will not stand in doubt; if you know Heaven and know Earth, you may make your victory complete."*

If the book could be summarized in one sentence, this would be that sentence. It covers all the bases, including the one we haven't discussed yet, self-knowledge. Knowing your enemy and the environment you're battling in would seem like the obvious things to do your pre-war homework on, not studying yourself. But why take the time to obtain a deep knowledge of "you"? To answer that, the book explains that:

> *"Knowing the enemy enables you to take the offensive, knowing yourself enables you to stand on the defensive."*

Meaning:

> *"If ignorant both of your enemy and yourself, you are certain to be in peril."*

In other words, the more you know yourself, the less ignorant you will be, which, in the case of losing battles, is anything but blissful. All of the war-mongering advice in the Art of War can translate into a life with almost no mongering going on. But self-awareness certainly seems to be the key.

Though Sun Tzu might not have been a real person, whoever wrote the Art of War was meant to inspire their readers to achieve great things. His inspiration is his work. Not the other way around. And that's what makes this chapter truly unique, not that the person might not have existed, but that the thing that he/they created is inspiration at its finest.

CHAPTER 7

Genghis Khan
(1155/1162 – 1227)

Warrior / Conqueror / Ruler of the Mongolian Empire

"Those who were adept and brave fellows I have made military commanders. Those who were quick and nimble I have made herders of horses. Those who were not adept I have given a small whip and sent to be shepherds"

  - Genghis Khan

Genghis Khan, before he became one of the greatest world conquerors of all time, was born and raised into a nomadic clan in the hills and mountains of Mongolia around 1155 AD. Unfortunately, most historians have been unable to dig up any specific characteristics of Genghis as a child other than a few objectively terrible early life events.

After Khan's father died, his family was swept into poverty and had to scrounge around the hills looking for animal carcasses to feed their tribe. Despite these setbacks, Khan was able to win a few skirmishes against enemy tribes and establish himself as a leader of men and a cunning general. Khan's family was at war during his early attempts at power. Through many literal family feuds, Genghis was able to take control of his family's assets as well as his wife's family's, making him a wealthy figure in the Mongolian Nomadic community.

From there, Genghis worked hard to unite the many nomadic tribes of Mongolia. That was his goal before he became a Euro-Asiatic conqueror. History shows us that these tribes, or confederations as they were called, constantly fought and warred with each other. However, Genghis saw the potential the confederacies had if only they would unite and fight together. His vision was spot on.

Through his vision, Genghis brought them together and created a code called Yassa. It was meant to be a civilian and military code designed to make the Empire more efficient and orderly. Needless to say, Yassa worked.

Power

Throughout his life, Khan was always seeking power, even in his romantic life, though having many wives and concubines was common for ruling classmen at the time. Though he started out his married life at nine years of age to only one girl named Borte, Genghis would go on to shack up hundreds if not thousands of women.

Geneticists estimate that Genghis has over 16 million living descendants today. Some have reported that the emperor had around 40 sons, although the number is most likely higher. Khan had multiple wives, main concubines, and other minor concubines at his disposal.

Interestingly enough, they weren't just eye candy for Genghis's excessively compulsive pleasure. They also served as assistants in ruling his vast empire, which, in its heyday, spanned from Eastern Europe to Japan, up to southern Russia, and down to northern India. To maintain a mass of land that large, Genghis relied on not just his generals but his lady friends as well. Even in love, Genghis was tactful.

In governance of his empire, Genghis was even more tactful. Through his great intellect, Khan invented a system designed around merit, essentially allowing groups under his rule to administer themselves. The system was innovative for its time, making Genghis much more than just a conqueror but a political and fiscal innovator. Including the style of governance he enforced throughout his empire, whose difficulty he respected:

> *"Conquering the world on horseback is easy; it is dismounting and governing that is hard."*

Genghis then devised a system that allowed him to keep conquering with his full force without having to expend too many soldiers for local governance. The system worked and Genghis was able to control his empire's extensive land holdings with a decent amount of stability. Genghis, his many children, and his loyal generals had a fearsome reputation. His acts of excessive violence and merciless cruelty were well known, most likely assisting the empire in keeping its subjects in a compliant state of mind.

Which is just another testament to the overall theme of Genghis Khan's life, that he is a master adjuster, a man who evolved and adapted to meet the incredible challenges of his time and circumstances. We can see his mindset clearly when Genghis says:

> *"Man's highest joy is in victory: to conquer one's enemies; to pursue them; to deprive them of their possessions; to make their beloved weep; to ride on their horses; and to embrace their wives and daughters"*

In pop culture, Genghis Khan is seen as a stereotypical 'hun,' an unsophisticated barbaric warrior who ravaged the world and destroyed cities instead of the intelligent leader he was. Partly because of comments like this one:

> *"A man's greatest joy is crushing his enemies."*

And:

> *"All who surrender will be spared; whoever does not surrender but opposes with struggle and dissension, shall be annihilated."*

History says (as well as Genghis himself) that the Mongolian conqueror was actually extremely cruel and merciless in his conquests. Some historians estimate that Genghis Khan and his generals were responsible for 10-15 million deaths. By comparison, the holocaust was responsible for the deaths of around 6 million Jews. With all of these deaths, Genghis Khan ranks among the most bloody and deadly figures in world history.

In all of his military campaigns, Genghis always found ways to win. During one battle, he even used the prisoners from the previous battle as human body shields.

Another military campaign inside the Khwarezmian Empire (modern Turkey and Iran) was caused by the empire refusing to trade with the Mongols, so Genghis launched a siege on their trade cities. Genghis had sent out some of his officials to make an agreement with the Khwarezmians. But they rudely refused, and Genghis launched an all-out assault on the three main cities of the Khwarezmian Empire. When the fighting was finished, Genghis held two of the main cities and most of the empire's aristocracy, the same people who refused to trade with him. We won't go into what Genghis did to them, only what he told them when they asked for mercy:

> **"If you had not committed great sins, God would not have sent a punishment like me upon you."**

Throughout the campaign, there were reports of mass killings, mainly of the Khwarazmian soldiers. However, modern archeology does not support these claims made by the officials documenting the events of the day.

The conquering of the Khwarezmian Empire is similar to many other military assaults Genghis carried out. Mainly in how destructive he was. His brutality was for a reason, though, as understood through this quote attributed to Genghis Khan himself.

"I am the punishment of God"

Those numbers and battle stories certainly don't paint a positive picture of Genghis. However, his accomplishments are still great. His legacy, even by history's standards, is a complicated bag of deeds that were both beneficial and harmful to humankind.

Economically, Genghis set up a trade system that gave birth to a more efficient Silk Road. This, in turn, fueled a booming international economy between China, Europe, and Arabia. Through all the bloodshed, Genghis created a lot of wealth for a lot of people, including himself.

In addition to upgrading an international economy, Genghis also practiced religious tolerance on his subjects. It was the standard belief of Mongolian culture that religious practice pertained to the individual's beliefs. Despite religion often being a vehicle in which to exercise control over subjects, Genghis never used religion to press his subjects. As mentioned before, Genghis had a very hands-off approach to governing his empire. Unlike, say, the Roman Empire who ruled their provinces with a stern iron fist that usually gripped a very sharp spear.

The same principle of merit also applied to the way Genghis structured his own government. Many kingdoms, empires, or civilizations were ruled via aristocrats. If a king needed a general, he would search amongst his best land-holding subjects and pick one to follow him into battle, or be his advisor, or be an administrator of some kind. Not Genghis. When the Mongol conqueror was assembling his government, he would often fill positions based on talent, work ethic, and overall merit of the individual. Pragmatically the system made sense, and by all accounts, Genghis was a very practical man. His love life was practical, his governance was unbiased, and his conquering was zero tolerance and no-nonsense.

All in all, Genghis Khan was a complicated figure, and as morally ambiguous as they come. But it is not our job as readers of history to study the past as a group of self-righteous moral police. If that's how you read history, then you're doing it wrong.

Genghis Khan is a perfect example of how one can rise from poverty, desolation, and hopelessness to become one of the greatest conquerors in all of history. Murdering aside, in modern times, he could be seen as an inspiration to entrepreneurs and athletes who wish to build great businesses and careers from nothing but their talents and elbow grease.

CHAPTER 8

Leif Erikson

(c 970 – c 1020)

Viking Explorer – First European to Discover North America

"We are all leaders-whether we want to be or not. There is always someone we are influencing - either leading them to good - or away from good."

- *Leif Erikson*

The Great Illusion of History

In the 1960s, archeologist Anne Stine Ingstad discovered a Norse site on the northern tip of modern-day Newfoundland. The site they found indicated that the people that lived there were not recent inhabitants but most likely Norse colonists from the 11th century. Further archeological searches revealed other settlements throughout the area that later Norse settlers had named Leifsbudir, or, in English, 'Leif's Booth.' The site, according to Norse sources, was named after Leif Erikson, or Leif the Lucky, as some called him. Even though Leifsbudir may not be the same site that Ingstad found, it proves one important thing: there were Europeans in the Americas half a millennium before Christopher Columbus. And not just that, but thanks to Norsemen like Leif the Lucky, many other medieval Norse people already knew of the North American continent.

There is an illusion that history has perpetuated for most of the 20th and 21st centuries that Europeans before 1492 had no inkling of what the Americas were, nor the people that lived there. But real history, not the curriculum taught in schools, says otherwise. And even though many of you know who Leif Erikson is, you probably don't know the extent of what he accomplished and the aftermath his discovery had on the Old World.

Exploration Roots

The primary historical sources we have that discuss Lief

are the Saga of Erik the Red and the Saga of the Greenlanders (as you can tell, they got really creative with book names), written around 1200 AD, or 180 years after the death of Leif. Erik the Red was Leif's father, hence the name 'Eriks-son,' and earned his nickname from his famous red hair and beard. He was also an explorer, like many wealthy Norsemen in that century.

Both Erik and Leif's ancestors had been exploring and colonizing nearby land for the seafaring Norse, who were always looking for a new place to expand their economic reach. One of the major first lands they colonized was Iceland, where many historians believe Leif was born. From there, they hopped over to Greenland (they were creative land name givers, too), with Erik the Red leading the way, and established a colony there, which is where Leif took off from when he discovered the Americas.

It might surprise you to know that some historical sources claim that there was a Nordic man who discovered the Americas before Leif. The claim begins with a merchant being blown off course and ends with his seeing off in the distance an unfamiliar shoreline. However, the merchant did not sail any closer. Instead, he turned around and got back on course. This claim is heavily disputed but shows how intensely Norse culture valued exploration and, most importantly, colonization. It was their bread and butter. 400 years before the Spanish, Portuguese, French, and English ever colonized an inch of the Americas, or anywhere for that matter, the Norse people were colonizing the lands beyond them, turning them into settlements and growing their influence. And if the story about the merchant is true, perhaps he saw the Americas before Leif Erikson did. But they had yet to step foot on the continent that would become the Americas until Leif found it.

In the tradition of both explorers before and after him (looking at you, Columbus), he found the Americas by accident. On the day he made his discovery, Leif was on his way to preach the gospel message of Christianity to indigenous people in Greenland, of all things.

Religious Conflict
An interesting fact about Leif Erikson was that he did not worship Odin. In fact, the primary reason that Erikson was near the Americas had a lot to do with his Christianity. Leif was a staunch Christian in contrast to his father, who detested the new religion and was not at all pleased that his son had taken it up. And, to the chagrin of Erik, Leif even went on missions to convert the indigenous people of the Northern Americas. Or at least try to.

His journey towards Christianity had begun when the King of Norway converted him to the Roman Catholic faith currently sweeping the continent, leading Leif to turn around and convert his family (excluding Erik, of course).

The importance of Leif's faith played a major factor in the discovery and colonization of the Americas by the Norse people. Without his innate desire to share his newfound faith with the indigenous populations of the so-called New World, Leif may not have returned to the area as quickly and passionately as he did.

According to the sagas, Leif found the Americas, looked around, rescued someone from a shipwreck, and then turned around back towards Greenland to evangelize the indigenous people there. Then Leif is said to have gathered up a crew of 35 men and returned to a land he dubbed Vinland. He describes the land as being filled with 'self-sown wheat' and 'grapevines,' though these descriptions may be exaggerated. Leif also found indigenous people in this new mysterious land.

Encounter with the Indigenous People

The initial encounters with the Inuit people of the far Northern regions were peaceful and productive. There were two different types of people that the Norsemen came in contact with, whom they had some very outdated names for. The sagas make the distinction between a "red-skinned" Indian and the Inuit, whom they affectionately referred to as the Nordic equivalent of "wretches." Despite their crude view of the indigenous populations, Leif and his men began trade relationships with the natives and probably tried to minister to them as well. However, all good things must come to an end, especially when language barriers are involved. Relations soured when Leif's brother, Thorvald, was struck with an arrow by an Inuit during a fight. If anything will make you mad at someone, it's when they shoot your brother with an arrow, and even more so when the wound ends up being fatal. The sagas describe the event of Thorvald's death with plenty of drama; for example, they wrote that he said, ironically, *"This is a rich country we have found; there is plenty of fat around my entrails."* Those, according to the sagas, were his last words. After Thorvald's death, the Norsemen continued to colonize the areas which scholars believe consisted of the East coast of modern-day Canada. During those days, however, it was known to Norsemen far and wide as Vinland. The sagas, after all, were written in Norway.

Further Explorations

They go on to describe much more than just interactions with the Inuit people. After Leif landed in Vinland, he took it upon himself to explore as much of it as he could. He set out with a crew of 35 men, though it was supposed to be 36 if Leif's father, Erik the Red, had been able to come. Perhaps the story would have been different if Erik had sailed along, but unfortunately, he had fallen off his horse recently, sustaining a bedridden injury in the process. In Norse culture, contracting that type of injury before a voyage was considered a bad omen, leaving Leif on his own and possibly cursed to explore the coast of this new land.

However, the first place they landed in was rather disappointing to the Norsemen, who were looking for plentiful land to settle. He was supposed to be following the borderline mythical Bjarni's route in reverse, which put them right alongside the modern-day Baffin islands or the far northern regions of Labrador. Both regions could be described like the Norsemen did, as a flat rock land, meaning there was not much potential to grow crops and achieve other means of survival. So, they moved on to their next landing spot, which turned out to be a completely different type of landscape than before. Scholars believe Leif and his crew landed in the heavily wooded area of Cape Porcupine on Labrador. But Leif dubbed the area Markland. Despite the promise the land offered through its ample supply of lumber, Leif did not stay docked there for very long. Two days after landing in Cape Porcupine, Leif and his crew island hopped a little bit longer before sailing west to the mainland, where they would finally settle down for the winter. Upon landing, Leif commanded his crew to go explore the area around where they were docked. One crew member named Tyrker found that the land was covered in grapevines, and when he reported his findings to Leif, the name Vineland, or Vinland, seemed to fit perfectly. It was in Vinland that the Norse branched out and established more settlements, becoming the first Europeans to colonize the Americas 500 years before the Spanish, English, or French ships even took off across the Atlantic during the age of exploration.

However, the medieval colonization that Leif led had a relatively widespread and virtually unknown effect on medieval and early modern Europe that no one ever talks about. Columbus is typically the explorer people credit with bringing knowledge of indigenous populations in the 'New World' to the attention of Europeans. But, in fact, that credit should go to Leif the Lucky.

Historians believe that upon Leif's return to Norway, word of the Americas' previously unknown existence spread throughout the ports of Northern Europe. Some even think that Columbus probably had heard about the discoveries on his visit to Iceland in 1477. And before that, in 1420, Danes captured Inuit people along with their kayaks, which they put on display in a Cathedral for curious Europeans to see.

Leif's legacy is a lot more important and far-reaching than many people presume it is. That's not including everything he had to overcome to make a major discovery, especially considering his famous voyage was cursed from the start. Overall, Leif the Lucky is an incredible explorer who changed the world through his discoveries, showing us that with a little luck and perseverance, anyone can make a profound discovery about our world.

CHAPTER 9

Mahatma Gandhi

(1869 – 1948)

Indian Lawyer / Anti-Colonial Nationalist / Political Ethicist

"An eye for eye only ends up making the whole world blind."

- Mahatma Gandhi

Gandhi's first taste of political activism was in South Africa, a surprising fact given his well-known association with India. But it was in South Africa where Gandhi initially had activism literally beaten into his brain by an officer enforcing a segregation law against non-whites. This beating occurred after Gandhi refused to sit on the floor of a stagecoach next to the driver instead of the usual riding cab in the back. An officer was called and proceeded to throw the then young man off of the vehicle and beat him for his disobedience. Gandhi had wrapped up a part of his identity in himself being a Briton, making the treatment he received from those he perceived as 'Brits' very insulting and immoral. All in all, Gandhi spent 21 years in the extremely racially segregated cities of South Africa, cultivating a new political vision for his home country of India. He returned to the British colony of India with hopes of using the skills he learned abroad to free his home country.

Before he became the Gandhi we know today, the bald old man with skinny legs wearing a white loincloth, living in poverty to peacefully protest British Colonial rule. It is an iconic image. Commonly found in pop culture and inspirational Facebook quote memes. However, in Gandhi's London and South Africa days, most of us wouldn't recognize him at all. In those days, the future loin-clothed activist dressed in a suit, wore British clothes, and lacked his signature mustache. This complete fashion 180 was in part due to the very un-western upbringing Gandhi had and the career he chased after in his younger years.

Early life
He was born in Porbandar, British India, on October 2nd, 1869, to a politically active father. His family had long been involved in Indian politics. For example, Gandhi's father's job was minister to the local prince of Porbandar. But Gandhi's family, nevertheless, was very ingrained in Indian culture. When his father died, Gandhi, who had already been married for three years, left home at the age of 16 to become a lawyer to support his family. To really fulfill his desire to be a Briton, he studied in London and embraced the culture. Though, due to a promise made to his mother, Gandhi still abstained from eating meat, drinking alcohol, and fooling around with English women.

That promise was the only way he could attain her blessing to study law in London, and the trade-off worked. Though Gandhi had been excommunicated from his caste for betraying his culture in such a way, showing how deeply rooted in traditional Indian culture Gandhi was before he left for South Africa, this is where his political activism career would begin. Gandhi mainly fought for his fellow Indians living in South Africa, although fought may not be the best word to use. Throughout his career fighting for people's rights, Gandhi fought authority without laying a hand on them. His pacifist beliefs restricted Gandhi from hurting anyone. This life philosophy led to Gandhi being beaten on several occasions. He might as well have been a professional MMA fighter who wasn't allowed to strike back at his opponent.

During those 21 years Gandhi spent away from India in South Africa, he used his legal experience to help organize groups to protest against the oppressive South African government. In the process, Gandhi was spit on, called several racist names, and, you guessed it, beaten. However, Gandhi's early activism was tailored around a rather crooked perspective, at least to our modern minds. Gandhi's thinking was that Indians should be treated better than black South Africans. His reasoning followed the logic that Indian people were closer in race to the Aryans and should therefore be treated better than the black Africans. Later on in his South African stay, however, Gandhi lent his support to blacks all over the continent of Africa. He showed support for the Zulus when the Empire waged war against them. And Nelson Mandela would later say that Gandhi and his supporters were there to help them during the early part of the Apartheid years.

Return to India
When Gandhi returned to India, he was a new man. After leading a group of volunteers in the Zulu war, and seeing how criminally and obnoxiously awful the British were to their colonial subjects, Gandhi realized that any kind of civil cooperation would not suffice. Meaning that Gandhi's gloves were off, even though he did not wear gloves, making the philosophical change all the more serious. The way British soldiers had shot his volunteers while they attempted to treat the wounded Zulu during battle solidified this newfound attitude.

In 1915, Gandhi found himself in another British Colony where a culture, his culture, and his people were being oppressed for financial gain benefitting an Empire across the world. At least, that is how Gandhi saw it. His return had actually been a request from the leadership of the Indian National Congress, a group of rebels seeking independence from Britain, who wanted Gandhi's internationally known community organizing skills and patriotism. Four years later, Gandhi told the Viceroy of India that if they did not pass a piece of legislation called the Rowlatt Act, he would direct the people of India to practice civil disobedience. As adorable as Gandhi was, this threat was very serious. By that point, Gandhi had become one of the leading voices for Indian Nationalism in the colony. His philosophy had won over the people, and many were ready to take up the call to action with him regardless of the dangerous consequences.

In 1920, Gandhi became the head of the Indian National Congress, solidifying his position as leader of the independence movement in India. Now he could fully implement his revolutionary philosophy and help push Congress to achieve its goal of Indian freedom. But what is Gandhi's 'philosophy'?'

Hind Swaraj

For the past several paragraphs, I've mentioned Gandhi's philosophy many times without telling you precisely what that philosophy is. If you want to understand Gandhi, you need to understand the reason he championed being uncooperative instead of practicing diplomacy. Gandhi's methods, and the reasoning behind them, can all be found in his book *Hind Swaraj*, which translates to English as India Home. The activist sums up Indians' conditions in this passage, as well as reminding them what freedom is:

"We measure the universe by our own miserable foot-rule. When we are slaves, we think that the whole universe is enslaved. Because we are in an abject condition, we think that the whole of India is in that condition. As a matter of fact, it is not so, yet it is as well to impute our slavery to the whole of India. But if we bear in mind the above fact, we can see that if we become free, India is free. And in this thought you have a definition of Swaraj. It is Swaraj when we learn to rule ourselves."

In another passage, Gandhi provides the solution:

"Passive resistance is a method of securing rights by personal suffering, it is the reverse of resistance by arms."

It is the passive resistance that will win the day, according to Gandhi. Remember, he was a pacifist and had been his whole life. Despite being a revolutionary, Gandhi did not believe the best method to overthrow a ruler was, as he calls it, *"resistance by arms."* In other words, the British subjugation of Indian citizens depended on the latter's civil cooperation; take away that cooperation, and the Brits would lose control over India. It's the same principle that Flick and the ants in *A Bug's Life* realize when they finally fight back against the oppressive mafia-esque grasshoppers. Except, in Gandhi's case, literal fighting was not an option. Not unless one considers fasting to be a form of combat, then yes, Gandhi was a fasting warrior. Simply not eating was one of the activist's main strategies to get the attention of British lawmakers and officials. As a result of constantly starving himself, Gandhi's body became very gaunt and scrawny. We've probably all seen an iconic image of the man, chest exposed, and every bone seen through dirt-covered skin. Now you know the context behind those startling pictures.

However, despite his starved appearance, Gandhi was still relatively healthy, even up to the point when India was on the verge of a potential civil war, while Gandhi was pushing the age of 77 in 1946. That year, though India was close to finally attaining independence, their revolution was extremely divided. The dividing line was religion, a battle between Muslim Indians and Hindi Indians. Gandhi had to solve the problem of a two-headed dragon, all without a single sword to speak of. By then, however, Gandhi had used his law degree to become quite a skilled politician. In 1947 the British began to broker independence and relative peace between his Hindi Congress and the Muslim League. When Britain finally released India in 1947, they left behind a carved-up and discombobulated nation. (A trademark of British Colonialism was disregarding the ethnic diversity of their colonial subjects when dividing up formerly colonized land.) For example, when Britain gave India back, they organized it into two countries, India and Pakistan.

Though Gandhi initially wanted a fully unified India, he ended up with a divided one instead. Like a kid who got cool stuff for Christmas but not the big thing he or she wanted, the cool toy from the commercials. Despite this bittersweet ending, Gandhi, on India's first Independence Day, instructed his fellow Indians to act peacefully and not fight over their new freedom. Some scholars credit Gandhi's call for peace as a positive catalyst in the transition of power in the newly free India.

Sadly, Gandhi did not get to enjoy seeing his dreams of a free India finally come to fruition for very long. On January 30th, 1948, less than a year after independence, Gandhi was assassinated by a Hindu Nationalist. To understand the effect Gandhi's death had on the people of India, this radio announcement by their newly elected Prime Minister sums it up well:

> *"Friends and comrades, the light has gone out of our lives, and there is darkness everywhere, and I do not quite know what to tell you or how to say it. Our beloved leader, Bapu as we called him, the father of the nation, is no more."*

Gandhi's life can be broken to a level of resilience rarely found in a human being. He worked hard for over 40 years, taking on one of the biggest and most powerful political forces in the world, the British Empire. And not once did he deviate from his pacifist, non-cooperative protest methods for four decades. If anyone lives out this kind of dedication and focus, the skies the limit, especially if that sky is toppling an Empire.

I leave you with some final quotes by the great man:

"Be the change that you wish to see in the world."

"The weak can never forgive. Forgiveness is the attribute of the strong."

"Nobody can hurt me without my permission."

"God has no religion."

"Each night, when I go to sleep, I die. And the next morning, when I wake up, I am reborn."

CHAPTER 10

Joan of Arc

(1412 – 1431)

Warrior / Saint

"I die for speaking the language of the angels."

- *Joan of Arc*

A young French peasant woman of about 19 is answering questions from powerful English clergymen. Their questions are designed to lead her to admit to a crime she certainly did commit, but contrary to modern perceptions and expectations, the crime is not witchcraft, which would have been the prototypical crime to charge a young woman with if you wanted her burned at the stake. Instead, the questions were trying to trick the young peasant woman into admitting to heresy (belief or opinion contrary to orthodox religious beliefs). However, upon asking questions like: *"if she knew she was in God's grace,"* to that loaded question the woman responded:

> **"If I am not, may God put me there; and if I am, may God so keep me. I should be the saddest creature in the world if I knew I were not in His grace."**

That was a very clever response to a question that should have sent her to the stake. If she had answered yes to the question, she would have claimed to know what God is thinking, which is heretical. Whereas, if she had answered no, then she would have confessed to falsely claiming that she knew God did not have her in his grace, which also happens to be a form of heresy. According to the records, the witnesses were astounded at the woman's many deflective responses to the English inquisitors. And the inquisitors were both flabbergasted and frustrated when the woman was deemed not guilty after her trial for heresy concluded and her trial for cross-dressing began. In 1431, dressing like the opposite gender was a crime. Once her enemies were able to prove that she had crossed dressed (it didn't help that she had cut her hair short like a man and refused to remove her masculine outfit while in jail), they convicted her and sentenced the young woman to burn at the stake. On May 30th, 1431, the pro-English clergy had Joan of Arc tied to a long wooden pillar, placed logs at her feet, and fulfilled her last request she made before they lit the fire. And so, a crucifix was held at sight level as she called out the name of Jesus with her last words.

It seems strange to a modern reader, who is probably familiar with the sexism of the Middle Ages, that the government of England and its "slightly" politically affiliated clergy would be so driven to convict a 19-year-old peasant woman. That is because even to medieval Europeans, the trial of Joan of Arc was odd.

Her story is like a fly floating around in a vat of milk. The milk is a white sea of medieval European records and tales about noblemen, high-ranking clergy, a few knights, and a wealthy commoner here and there. Meanwhile, the fly is Joan, who was born in the late Middle Ages in 1412 to the daughter of a farmer and not a wealthy one either. By medieval socio-economic standards, Joan was indeed a peasant, as previously described. For a peasant in the middle ages, there were only a few springboards available for them to jump classes. The primary method was joining the church and becoming a clergyman, while the second was the military. However, those avenues were generally closed off to women, with the exception of joining a nunnery. Under those circumstances, Joan had arguably the most difficult socio-economic achievement of all.

Nowadays, Joan of Arc is synonymous with feminism, revolution, and martyrdom. Without her revolutionary endeavors, however, the other legacies would not be possible. When Joan was a teenager, a conflict was raging through Western Europe between France and England. We know it today as the 100 Years War. Of course, the point at which Joan entered the war, no one called it that; it was simply a war for territory between two royal institutions who felt entitled to certain lands in Northern France. And perhaps the most famous figure to come out of this war was Joan.

Visions

Her story's inciting incident occurred when she was just 13. One day Joan was in her father's garden when she was suddenly struck with a powerful vision. She claims to have seen three saints, the great Saint Michael, Saint Catherine, and last but not least, Saint Margaret. Unfortunately, they were not there to have a nice chat. No, they were there to give Joan holy instructions. 13-year-old Joan listened to the trio of Saints giving her an important mission; to drive the English out of France and restore the prominence of France, which had, for centuries, been the most powerful semi-unified Kingdom in Europe.

Up to 1425, the year Joan claims to have had her visions, France was in a tough spot. In a post-Black Death Europe, the French region was not recovering as quickly as its peers were, partly because England's strategy of ravaging the rural population didn't help. The English, and their allies, the Burgundies, controlled the majority of Northern France, including Paris. Meanwhile, France had just anointed a new king who was making what seemed to be a sloppy attempt at waging war on their unwanted English guests.

Joan, three years after seeing her vision, at the age of 16, Joan asked a relative named Durand Lassois to take her to the French garrison commanded by a minor nobleman Robert De Baudricourt, where she petitioned the commander to give her an armed escort to the royal court in Chinon for an audience with the French king, Charles VII. Baudricourt, upon being asked for an audience with the king of France by an illiterate peasant girl, responded rather facetiously. However, Joan did not give up. Instead, she appealed to two of Baudricourt's soldiers, proclaiming to them that:

> *"I must be at the King's side ... there will be no help (for the kingdom) if not from me. Although I would rather have remained spinning [wool] at my mother's side ... yet must I go and must I do this thing, for my Lord wills that I do so."*

Upon hearing this, the two soldiers supposedly vouched

for the young peasant girl and got her another audience with Baudricourt. However, he was still hesitant to put his reputation on the line for what probably appeared to be a mentally ill farmer's daughter babbling on about visions and meeting the king. So, to prove her divine backing, Joan made a bold prediction. She predicted that the Battle of Herrings would take an unexpected turn, and sure enough, Baudricourt received a message that fit Joan's prediction perfectly. Now a reluctant believer, Baudricourt accepted Joan's request and took on her divine quest to see Charles VII.

Baudricourt assembled an armed escort headed for Chinon, with Joan disguised as a male soldier wearing military garb exclusive to men (like a French Mulan of sorts.) Though it was necessary to armor up when traveling through 15th-century France, this would be the decision that sent her to the stake 3 years later.

Joan was 17 when she met Charles VII, who was only 26 himself. They were two young people with a lot to prove to their constituents, all while struggling to do so the majority of the time. During their first meeting, Charles VII was intrigued by Joan and her claims of divine providence. And conveniently, Joan's arrival coincided with a possible turning point in the siege of Orleans, which prior to Joan of Arc's arrival had been going very poorly for the French. Charles's mother-in-law Yolande of Aragon was already heading to Orleans to provide financial aid when Joan asked to tag along. Her answer was yes. While this may be beginning to sound like a fairytale. A peasant girl gets an audience with royalty and is brought along with the French dressed like a man so they can use her as a holy good luck charm. In reality, Joan's story is less fairy and more political than it appears.

Joan of Arc Historian Stephen W. Richey observed, *"only a regime in the final straits of desperation would pay any heed to an illiterate farm girl who said that the voice of God was instructing her to take charge of her country's army and lead it to victory."* Put another way, Joan became a religious and nationalistic symbol for the rebirth of France.

If you recall Joan's execution, there was a significant amount of foreshadowing of what she would become over time, not just to France but to an entire religion. After the fire had taken Joan's life, the executors decided to burn any remnants of her and reignited her corpse until she was nothing but ashes. The reason for this excessive amount of burning was to keep anyone taking home a relic, which would not bode well for the Catholic clergy, who wanted to avoid being known as the ones who martyred Joan of Arc. Despite their best efforts, however, that is exactly who they ended up becoming. Over the centuries, Joan has gained more and more attributes to her Sainthood. Even becoming the 9th Patron Saint of the nation of France. And for good reason.

Predictions and Strategic War Advice

Joan had made another bold prediction that her divine presence would help lift the siege and result in a French victory, the first significant one in a long time. When

Joan reached the siege of Orleans, the battle seemed to immediately reverse the French's previously dire fortunes. The French leaders included noblemen such as Jean d'Orleans and the Duke of Alencon. As time went on, Joan eventually gained their trust. At Jargeau, the battle that followed the siege at Orleans, the Duke of Alencon claims that Joan warned him that a cannonball had fired, so he had time to maneuver out of its path. In addition to her leadership, Joan also proved to the war-worn military men that she could handle the arbitrary violence of combat. During the siege, while holding up her banner, Joan was struck with an arrow between her neck and shoulder, as well as absorbing a blow from a projectile rock to her helmet, but she did not allow the injuries to impede her providential enthusiasm.

Joan quickly went from being shunned at military meetings by the aristocratic war leaders to gaining their respect (or as much respect as noblemen in the Middle Ages could afford to an illiterate peasant girl). They also testified that Joan had been very helpful in giving them strategic advice, despite having no prior experience in warfare. Both previously mentioned noblemen attest to not only listening and acting on Joan's suggestions but allocated her credit for them. Not long after the victory at Orleans, the French had the opportunity to strike again, with the expectation that they would attempt to retake their beloved city of Paris. To further assist her country, Joan offered an aggressive and risky strategy that Charles VII agreed to act on. Charles, along with many other French noblemen, believed that God had sent Joan of Arc to them as a sign that he supported them from the heavens. Not to mention her results spoke for themselves.

Post Orleans siege, the French went on the voracious offensive through Northern France, led by Joan. She helped them take back three different regions before being captured by Burgundian forces while traveling to Compiegne to assist in defending the city against an English siege. She tried to escape many times, including leaping from a 70ft high tower, before the English put her on trial for illegally dressing like a man, which was the one charge of many that finally stuck. The subsequent phony trial and martyr-like execution produced the currently held Joan of Arc image, the heroine who beat the system. Today she is known as someone who broke so many barriers, even if she was being used by the French nobility. She convinced and led such an exclusive group of people in one of the most exclusive socio-economic climates in history.

Joan of Arc was an aggressive military commander who always opted for offense instead of defense. In thirteen known engagements, her troops were victorious nine times. At least thirty different cities, towns, and villages surrendered without a fight when she approached with her army. Her fame only increased after her death, however, and 20 years later, a new trial ordered by Charles VII cleared her name. Long before Pope Benedict XV canonized her in 1920, Joan of Arc had attained mythic stature, inspiring numerous works of art and literature over the centuries and becoming the patron saint of France. In 1909 Joan of Arc was beatified in the famous Notre Dame cathedral in Paris by Pope Pius X. A statue inside the cathedral pays tribute to her legacy.

I will again leave you with some of her most inspirational quotes:

> *"How else would God speak to me, if not through my imagination?"*

> *"All battles are first won or lost, in the mind."*

> *"I am not afraid; I was born to do this."*

> *"Go forward bravely. Fear nothing. Trust in God; all will be well."*

INTERLUDE

At this point in the book, I have a small favor to ask. As A smaller author in a huge genre, I have learned that gathering reviews are hugely important to us.

If you like what you have read so far, and it has brought some value and perspective to your life, it would help me out immensely if you could take 30 seconds of your time and head over to Amazon and write a nice brief review. A sentence or two will do!

Just scan the relevant QR code with your phone camera, and it will take you straight there.

US: **UK:**

Thank you! I can't wait to see your thoughts.

<u>CHAPTER 11</u>

Charles Ponzi
(1882 – 1949)

Italian Swindler and Con Artist

"I landed in this country with $2.50 in cash and $1 million in hopes, and those hopes never left me."

- *Charles Ponzi*

I'm sure this isn't the first bio of Charles Ponzi that begins with this quote. It's a sincere quote from a relatively insincere guy who is famous for creating a method of financial theft that is still used today. In 2008, amongst many other financial catastrophes, the world discovered that "American Financier" Bernie Madoff had been running one of the biggest Ponzi schemes in market history. And yes, those were sarcastic air quotes. Because Madoff was as much of an investing genius as I am an octopus. Madoff started a penny stock firm in the 60s that grew into a full-blown fund that attracted the likes of Steven Spielberg and Henry Kaufman, an economist, amidst dozens and dozens of banks from every corner of the earth. Billions were lost. All due to the Ponzi scheme, conceived around 15 years before Madoff was even born, forever making the concept his, an eternal badge of dishonor.

Early Life

Charles Ponzi was born in Italy on March 3rd, 1882, to what he describes as a 'well to do' family that supposedly carried minor titles like Donna, a name he claims his mother could still use.

On November 15th, 1903, after arriving in Boston, a land where the young Ponzi felt he could make a name for himself. Charles had heard from some of his friends that it was easy to get rich in America, so here he was, with nothing but $2.50 in cash to his name. With his lack of capital and experience, Ponzi had to take on a series of odd jobs to make ends meet.

When he finally got a job at a local restaurant washing dishes, Ponzi had not only found a home (he's reported to have slept there after work) but the beginning of his scamming career. Not long after Ponzi proved to be a hard worker, the managers of the restaurant hired him as a waiter. A job he did pretty well, except for all the stealing and cheating. After Ponzi was fired, he continued to struggle to find work and save what little money he made. In other words, the workforce seemed to be ill-suited for Ponzi's creative spirit.

In an effort to get a break, Ponzi moved up to Montreal, Canada, in 1907. Ponzi's first job was as a teller for a new bank called Banco Zarossi, finally giving him a glimpse into how the financial system works in North America. Ponzi was eventually promoted to bank manager, in part due to him learning English and becoming far more confident, giving the young money seeker a close-up look at how the bank was really functioning. The capital the bank had received from its customers was all tied up in bad real estate assets and not being used to pay the bank's gloriously high-interest rate of 6%, which was irresponsibly being paid through new account deposits. Very dangerous. Essentially meaning that the bank would not be able to keep up with those high interest and be forced to default on their loans to their customers. Which is very illegal.

First Arrests
In the end, Zarossi ran away to Mexico with some stolen

money from the bank—while Ponzi was arrested and sent to prison for forging a check from the now-abandoned bank for over $400. Ponzi was caught because his high dollar purchases seemed suspicious to authorities investigating the bank's activity.

He spent 3 years in the pen and, like most convicts, only learned how to commit more crimes while inside. Ponzi befriended several other con-artists and criminals who taught him other ways of making money when he got out. And the second he eventually got out, Ponzi started smuggling illegal Italian immigrants (yes, white people can be illegal aliens too) and landed himself right back in a prison cell, this time in Atlanta.

He would spend two years there before being released in 1911. When he got out, Ponzi returned to Boston and worked a short stint trying to run honest businesses and miserably failed. One, in particular, was his wife's fruit stand. Yes, Ponzi convinced someone to marry him despite his brightly colored criminal record. However, Ponzi's efforts to help his wife and her family run their fruit stand were fruitless (sorry couldn't resist a good fruit pun), leading Ponzi to seek income elsewhere for his family.

The Origins of the Ponzi Scheme
In 1919 he found it. One day, while looking to sell business ideas, Ponzi received a letter with a document he had never seen before, an international reply coupon, or for short, an IRC. To most people during those days, this would not have sparked an idea to make millions of

legal dollars, for once. But most people are not Charles Ponzi, thank the gods.

To Ponzi, these IRCs posed a huge opportunity to exploit some weaknesses in the currency exchange network. What Ponzi found in the IRCs were some arbitrage stamps, meaning that stamps sent from Italy or Spain were worth less than the postage stamps in the U.S where Ponzi lived, so he could buy stamps in Italy, exchange them in America at higher currency rates, and turn a profit with ease. The concept is called arbitrage. Currently, millions of people use arbitrage to make profits on exchanges all around the world. But no one uses arbitrage stamps. The idea seemed perfect on paper, and Ponzi felt really strongly that the idea would attract investors looking for an easy legal way to make passive income through high-profit margin trades. The real question for Charles Ponzi was how to get those investors to give him their money.

Being familiar with Wall Street, Ponzi decided the best and most sure method to raise capital was through selling equities or stocks of his nonexistent trading firm, as well as offering high-interest rates to anyone who invested $1,250. The rates he was offering were around 50%, 45% higher than any of the banks in those days were offering. Not to mention he promised that they would double their money on their investment due to the ease at which the IRCs could be exchanged. Despite his past, Ponzi did follow through with all of his promises to his investors and built himself a sturdy reputation in the process.

Of course, there was only one problem. The arbitrage business couldn't possibly work. The IRCs can be exchanged, yes, but converting them to cash on a massive scale was simply impossible. Regardless, Ponzi kept receiving investment money from eager people looking to make a quick buck, paying off half their initial investment, then pocketing the other half.

It was, after all, 1920, the year that started off one of the most financially irresponsible decades in American history. Millions of people wanted to get in on the rising markets and the booming post-war economy. Ponzi was the man selling them their boom-boom dreams, one fake interest payment at a time.

As the economy went up, so did the investments. Ponzi began scaling his marketing efforts, starting by selling the modern equivalent of 32 million dollars a month worth of equities in his fake arbitrage business. However, Ponzi didn't want to completely bamboozle his investors. With all the cash flow he was accumulating, Ponzi had enough to buy a couple of different food manufacturing companies in the hopes that they would generate enough revenue to help pay back his victims.

Downfall

However, Ponzi was not quick enough. During the summer of 1920, the Boston Post began publishing articles investigating and analyzing the suspicious aspects of Ponzi's business model. They detailed how it would be impossible for him to even be able to ship that many IRCs and that even if they did, their profit margins would not be positive. Not to mention Ponzi wasn't even investing his profits back in the company. Instead, he was pumping it all into a bank, with the intent of eventually taking over the bank and single-handedly controlling the local economy (A+ for ambition). But soon, the articles caught on, and many people became suspicious of Ponzi and his exchange company.

The article that really did it for Ponzi was about how his company was in so much debt that it could not possibly be liquidated—meaning that the investors were screwed because their money was insolvent. After realizing this unfortunate truth, the investors made a run for the exchange company to try to get their cashback. And although Ponzi was able to pay off the people that demanded their money back, he still had to deal with the state banking commissioner investigating his accounts, which led to the commissioner finding out that Ponzi was $7 million in debt. He realized that the con artist was not only leveraging his investors but the bank he was trying to control. Therefore, if more runs were made on Ponzi's Exchange Company, the bank would have a major loan default situation on its hands. On top of that, the media only attacked him harder. They began a smear campaign against Ponzi, digging up some of the other schemes he had performed in the past as well as his many years in the pen.

It all happened so fast, like a roller coaster ride. In one fail swoop, the banking commissioner seized the bank Ponzi had been using, effectively ending his plans to leverage more money to pay back frantic investors, if you could call them that anymore.

Deportation

From there, Ponzi turned himself in and was convicted of dozens of counts of mail fraud and larceny over a period of years, eventually accumulating to around 12 years in prison before the feds got tired of housing him and deported him back to Italy.

In the judge's words:

> *"Here was a man with all the duties of seeking large money. He concocted a scheme which, on his counsel's admission, did defraud men and women. It will not do to have the world understand that such a scheme as that can be carried out ... without receiving substantial punishment."*

Before his deportation, Ponzi tried to escape by disguising himself as a bald mustached fellow and tried hopping on a boat to Italy. Sadly, Ponzi got caught in New Orleans and sent back to prison. That would be the last con he ever pulled again on American soil.

In Italy, Ponzi was still jumping from scheme to scheme, but nothing much came of it. He finally landed a job in Brazil as an agent for an Italian state airline. Unfortunately, the airline's operation in the country was shut down during World War II. He lived out his days in poverty in Brazil as his health declined rather rapidly until he died in Rio de Janeiro in 1949, leaving a complicated legacy behind in his wake.

Ponzi single-handedly took down 4 banks and cost his victims the modern equivalent of $190 million. He worked tirelessly to build his fake business and his bank takeover. Credit is due where credit is due; Ponzi was undoubtedly smart and had to think creatively like no one else had to before. His 'financial artistry' inspired Bernie Madoff and Jordan Belfort to create their own schemes, now known as a Ponzi scheme. And you can take inspiration from Ponzi too. Work hard, think outside the box, and do not, under any circumstances, sell fake investments.

CHAPTER 12

Fyodor Dostoevsky
(1821 – 1881)

Russian Novelist (Existentialism, Psychology, and more)

"The darker the night, the brighter the stars"

- Fyodor Dostoevsky

Fyodor was released from prison on Valentine's Day. His initial sentence included being executed via firing squad. Fortunately for Fyodor and western philosophy, the Tsar commuted his sentence. The punishment Dostoevsky received for his crimes was lowered to time in jail. What were Fyodor's crimes exactly? For reading a book. Technically it was a banned book, as well as being a member of a literary discussion group. The group discussed topics such as the abolishment of serfdom and freedom of speech. Some members even wrote books on the subjects. Serfdom was a condition in medieval Europe in which a tenant farmer was bound to a hereditary plot of land and to the will of his landlord. Fyodor was accused of reading a controversial book, reading a really controversial essay, and then distributing the said essay to other readers. The essays criticized the Russian government, leading authorities to suspect the group of being revolution inciters. For these perceived crimes, Dostoevsky served 4 years at a prison camp performing hard labor. After Fyodor was released, he didn't rejoin the group.

He did, however, write the first book about Russian prisons 6 years after his release. The novel was named the House of the Dead (can't you tell he had a blast there) and marked a big step in an iconoclastic direction, a path that Fyodor would follow for the rest of his life and career. It's a path that would seem unlikely for someone of his origin, which had more in common with Pride and Prejudice than Oliver Twist.

Early Years

Fyodor Dostoevsky was born in 1821 to a pair of parents who were, ironically, a facet of the serfdom problem in 19th-century Russia. They were not mega-wealthy by any means but could still afford young Fyodor a nanny and a library of books. Fyodor's nanny read him many stories, as did his parents. From the literature Fyodor read, he had a love for stories embedded in his young impressionable brain. In addition to reading stories, there are other aspects of Fyodor's childhood that made him the man he would become. One, specifically. One such event occurred when Fyodor had to report the rape of one of their family's 9-year-old serfs. This event would stay in Fyodor's psyche, possibly contributing to his comfort with discussing darker facets of humanity. His education didn't help much, either. Fyodor always struggled to find somewhere he belonged or where his parents could afford tuition.

Though his family was somewhat successful, they could barely afford to give him an education at a boarding school. And by the time Fyodor began attending military school, he had to appeal to other families for money. Military school would put Dostoevsky in a fish-out-of-water situation. Imagine throwing Bill Gates into the middle of a Marines training camp, and you'll get a basic picture of Fyodor in military school. While in school, Fyodor studied engineering and mathematics. However, his schoolmates complained that he disliked the hard sciences and observed him sneaking away to his room to read books on religion. Upon finishing military school, Fyodor began his career as an engineer. While working as a lieutenant engineer, Fyodor began a nasty combination of hobbies, translating books and gambling. In order to smooth over his money troubles and continue writing, Dostoevsky began work on a novel (which wasn't something considered to make money back then). Fortunately, Dostoevsky was particularly good at writing and became financially successful with his second novel, leading him to begin writing full-time. As any writer knows, however, writing full-time is like administering self-induced concussions every day. And not long after he began his new career, Dostoevsky began experiencing an uptick in seizures from his lifelong fight with epilepsy. (That was a joke about writing being like a concussion, and there is no evidence that writing full-time caused Dostoevsky's epilepsy to spike. On the other hand, the part about writing being comparable to self-afflicted concussions is very true).

Move towards Philosophy

Dostoevsky kept writing, even if some of his stories were commercial and critical duds. In the meantime, he was learning new ideas from circles of thinkers way outside of the influence of the military. Dostoevsky learned about ideas such as socialism, atheism, and class issues from several different thinkers of the day. The latter of which landed him in the prison camp.

When Dostoevsky was released, he did what anyone else would do, he asked his friend to send him books on philosophy. He also began his mandatory service in the Russian military as part of his sentencing. The philosophers he asked for include Hegel and Kant. Meaning that Dostoevsky might have been thinking about his existence. Though he was sickly and still in bad health, Dostoevsky wanted to understand the world around him and challenge his beliefs. One of his roommates described Fyodor as:

> *"he looked morose. His sickly, pale face was covered with freckles, and his blond hair was cut short. He was a little over average height and looked at me intensely with his sharp, grey-blue eyes. It was as if he were trying to look into my soul and discover what kind of man I was."*

After he released his novel about prison, Dostoevsky continued to publish stories and serve in the military. Until his health became so bad that he was released early in 1859, though it never stopped his writing, Dostoevsky's bad health destroyed his first marriage. Maria, his first wife, couldn't handle the stress that came with Dostoevsky's seizures and lack of money, and they spent part of their marriage in separation. I'm sure that was great for Fyodor's self-esteem. Their marriage ended with Maria's death in 1864. Commenting on his relationship with his first wife, Dostoevsky wrote:

"Because of her strange, suspicious and fantastic character, we were definitely not happy together, but we could not stop loving each other; and the more unhappy we were, the more attached to each other we became".

It is around this time that we shift to something very important in Dostoevsky's life, the book that would be his imprint on the world of philosophy, Crime, and Punishment. Fyodor Dostoevsky was an innovative writer throughout his career. He wrote the first book about life in a Russian prison. He published arguably the first 'social' book in Russian history. And, in the case of Crime and Punishment, Dostoevsky wrote a book about murder psychology, more or less. As with any work of literature, Crime and Punishment can be interpreted in various ways. (Spoilers Ahead). The books center around a man named Rodion Raskolnikov who is attempting to morally justify murdering a woman to whom he owes a lot of money. Rodion's justification for the murder he eventually carries out is partially summed up in this passage:

> *"In my opinion, if, as the result of certain combinations, Kepler's or Newton's discoveries could become known to people in no other way than by sacrificing the lives of one, or ten, or a hundred or more people who were hindering the discovery, or standing as an obstacle in its path, then Newton would have the right, and it would*

even be his duty... to remove those ten or a hundred people, in order to make his discoveries known to mankind. It by no means follows from this, incidentally, that Newton should have the right to kill anyone he pleases, whomever happens along, or to steal from the market every day. Further, I recall developing in my article the idea that all…well, let's say, the lawgivers and founders of mankind, starting from the most ancient and going on to the <u>Lycurguses</u>, the Solons, the Muhammads, the Napoleons, and so forth, that all of them to a man were criminals, from the fact alone that in giving a new law, they thereby violated the old one, held sacred by society and passed down from their fathers, and they certainly did not stop at shedding blood either, if it happened that blood (sometimes quite innocent and shed valiantly for the ancient law) could help them."

Is Rodion delusional? Or is he right? Is it his righteous duty to kill one measly person for the greater good? But what kind of greater good is Rodion even referring to? And this last question asked in the book: "What do you think, would not one tiny crime be wiped out by thousands of good deeds?"

These are the questions that make Crime and Punishment so profound. Of course, there's the incredible style Dostoevsky uses to write the story. Most books at the time followed a more linear descriptive style. However, Dostoevsky prefers to delve deep into his character's minds, as far into their psyche as he can go. For a novel like this, writing from a psychological perspective is what makes the story so effective. And when a story is effective, it is, in some way, real. Today, psychological thrillers like Fight Club and Gone Girl are commonplace. Next to them, the concepts of moral relativity are everywhere, and next door to them are moral dilemmas. However, when Dostoevsky initially wrote Crime and Punishment, he had more socio-political intentions. The book is more of a polemic against what Dostoevsky saw as a wayward Russia. He believed they were going in the wrong direction and wrote the novel to criticize the utilitarian thinking he saw permeating his country. It is innovative that instead of writing a journalistic piece or an essay, Dostoevsky chose to write a psychoanalytical novel.

After the publication of Crime and Punishment, which was released in installments like most books of the 19th century, Dostoevsky married his second wife, Anna. His relationship with her was much more stable and loving than his last marriage. It all started when Dostoevsky needed a secretary to help complete his next novel. As you can probably guess, Anna was Fyodor's secretary. The relationship was plagued with excessive debt achieved through consistent gambling performed by Dostoevsky. But Anna loved him. She stuck with him through thick and thin. When the earnings from Crime and Punishment came in the mail and weren't enough to cover Dostoevsky's debt, Anna sold some of her valuables to pay them off. Despite the gambling, his marriage to Anna provided some domestic stability for Dostoevsky. He continued to write and publish famous novels such as Idiot (yes, that's the name of the book), Diary, and The Brothers Karamazov, which would be his last completed work. In addition to novels, Dostoevsky also helped create some people, four people to be exact. On the surface, it may have seemed like a relatively happy marriage. However, in addition to the gambling, Dostoevsky had at least two known affairs. Though he only confesses to loving one of them.

Death

Living the life of a gambling ladies' man psychological novelist, Dostoevsky lived out the last years of his life large. However, always burdened with crappy health, Dostoevsky eventually succumbed to death in 1881 at the age of 59. The causes of Fyodor's death, surprisingly, had nothing to do with his epilepsy and were instead due to a pulmonary hemorrhage.

Since Dostoevsky was a religious man, he requested that his children be read the parable known as the Prodigal Son on his deathbed.

Dostoyevsky will be regarded as one of the greatest novelists who ever lived. Literary modernism, theology, existentialism, and various schools of psychology have been profoundly shaped by his ideas. There are many lessons to be learned from the life of Fyodor Dostoevsky. Lessons such as:

"Pain and suffering are always inevitable for a large intelligence and a deep heart.

The really great men must, I think, have great sadness on earth."

In other words, it's okay to be great and sad sometimes. Never forget that. To end on a more positive note, I leave you with some of the more uplifting quotes from this great mind:

"To go wrong in one's own way is better than to go right in someone else's."

"It takes something more than intelligence to act intelligently."

"Talking nonsense is the sole privilege mankind possesses over the other organisms. It's by talking nonsense that one gets to the truth! I talk nonsense, therefore I'm human"

"The mystery of human existence lies not in just staying alive, but in finding something to live for."

"We sometimes encounter people, even perfect strangers, who begin to interest us at first sight, somehow suddenly, all at once, before a word has been spoken."

CHAPTER 13

Sir Isaac Newton
(1643 – 1727)

Mathematician/Physicist/Astronomer

"I do not know what I may appear to the world; but to myself, I seem to have been only like a boy playing on the seashore, and diverting myself now and then in finding a smoother pebble or prettier shell than ordinary, while the great ocean of truth lay all undiscovered before me."

- *Sir Isaac Newton*

Ask anyone on the street how gravity was discovered, and they will tell you a story of an old powdered wigged scientist having an epiphany from watching an apple from a tree. This is the tale commonly associated with the famous scientist Sir Isaac Newton. And despite the story probably being false, it has made Newton a popular figure in pop culture. But that folksy portrait of Newton is not exactly an accurate representation of what Newton's life actually looked like. Perhaps a better image would be that of a rich, slightly mad scientist with an elegant 17th-century wig. If this Isaac Newton doesn't sound like the wise scientist sitting under the shady apple tree getting minor concussions, then that false perception is understandable. So often, iconic historical figures like George Washington or Cleopatra become caricatures of themselves. And Newton is no exception.

Early Life
You were also probably unaware that Newton was born on Christmas day in 1642 (though some historians aim at a slightly later date of January 4th, 1643). He was born in the town of Woolsthorpe-by-Colsterworth, a town in the county of Lincolnshire now famous for being the birthplace of Sir Isaac Newton. Records say that Newton was born prematurely, a much more dangerous prospect than it is considered today. Of course, Newton survived but was left behind by his widowed mother after she moved in with her new husband, a Reverend, when Isaac was just three years old, leaving Newton

behind to live with his maternal grandmother. And when he was 12 his mother sent him off to a school in Grantham. While attending the school, Newton developed a proclivity for the sciences, especially mathematics. However, his mother, in spite of his obvious intelligence, demanded that her son quit school and become a farmer (the opposite of what parents want in the 21st century). Fortunately for science and humanity, the master of the school in Grantham convinced Newton's mother that the young genius should stay in school.

From there, Newton attended Cambridge University, at least until the institution was temporarily closed due to the plague, something we can relate to in the 21st century. Despite the setback of not having a school to study at, Newton started formulating various theories and laws centered around gravity, among many other mathematical subjects. Newton also dabbled in optics, where he developed a sophisticated theory on the spectrum of color. However, it was ultimately Newton's theories on gravity that would etch his name in the history books.

Gravity

In his book Principia, Newton formulated his theories on math and gravity on paper for all the world to see (at least those who could read, which in those days was a small portion of the population). Many of the scientific laws we know of today are found in Principia. And one thing you must know about Isaac Newton is that he created a lot of laws. The most famous, of course, are the three laws of gravity that Newton developed in his younger years. But exactly what are laws in the scientific sense? Similar to the laws that regulate our society, the laws that Newton discovered are rules for how the various components of things like *motion* works in the empirical world. For example, one of Newton's laws of motion states that an object in motion will stay in motion unless stopped by another force. While this may seem obvious to us now, it is quite profound when you consider that it took humans millennia to finally quantify the laws of motion. Nowadays, we have the privilege of saying phrases like "whoa! Fred just defied the laws of physics!" whenever something unexplainable happens. The laws have stood the test of time due to Newton's incredible math skills, which also led to revolutionary work in other subjects like calculus (if you've ever had to take a calculus class, you have Newton to thank).

It is ironic that Newton discovered gravity due to a belief in the occult (the supernatural). During the 17th century, enlightenment ideas were sweeping the fields of science, philosophy, and concepts of government. The main driver behind this movement was reasoning, specifically empirical reasoning. Though Newton was a catalyst of the enlightenment movement, he faced controversy from his peers with his theory on gravity which used the traditionally occult concept of action at a distance to explain the invisible force known as gravity. Today, of course, Newton's gravitational laws are understood to be scientific and certainly not occultic. And if not for the occult belief that inanimate objects can move by themselves, Newton may never have had the idea to mathematically formulate the concept of gravity. But because Newton did go against his peers, future physicists like George Lemaitre and Albert Einstein had a mathematical foundation to build on when it came to theoretical physics, the latter of which had a framed portrait of Newton that always sat on his work desk.

The Alchemist

You may already be familiar with this information, but you probably were not aware that Newton was an alchemist. In our modern world, what Newton called alchemy or chymistry, we now call chemistry.

Despite alchemy's popularity in 17th-century Europe, many people in England had no idea that Newton conducted as many experiments as he did. Scholars estimate that around 10% of Newton's writings are about alchemy, making it a relatively large portion of his studies that virtually no one knows about (and for good reason.) Because all throughout his life, Newton hid his alchemy experiments. As fiction writer Fritz Leiber brazenly says: *"Everyone knows Newton as the great scientist. Few remember that he spent half his life muddling with alchemy, looking for the philosopher's stone. That was the pebble by the seashore he really wanted to find."*

And more often than not, he was completely alone in his alchemy endeavors. Many of his written works on alchemy were very cryptic in their descriptions, not revealing anything specific that a reader could copy. In other words, Newton didn't want anyone else to learn about his alchemy discoveries. Although it is not clear whether or not Newton was after Nicholas Flamel's philosopher's stone, it is quite obvious Newton was conducting alchemical experiments.

As it so happens, when Newton died in 1727, a sample of hair was extracted from his head, and when subsequently tested, it was found to have traces of mercury in it, a highly toxic chemical. Scholars believe that the reason Newton had so much mercury in his hair was due to his alchemy experiments.

Outside Science

Even in his 80s, Newton was still trying to make new scientific discoveries. However, science was not the only aspect of Newton's life. Away from science, Newton enjoyed the lifestyle of a wealthy Brit, despite being of common and middle-class birth. Due to his patronage from a powerful English aristocrat, Newton was given a high position at the Royal Mint, where he accrued a substantial amount of money. Newton invested in the South Sea Company but lost 20,000 pounds after the company collapsed in 1720, the modern equivalent of over 4 million pounds.

In the process of becoming wealthy (and losing some of it), Newton also played politics. Queen Anne, the last British ruler from the House of Stuart, knighted Newton with the more likely intention of boosting his reputation before his attempt at joining parliament, which was a position he probably could not have imagined when he was a young boy living with his grandmother. Or even when he first released his defining book Principia.

Perseverance

By all accounts, Newton had to overcome a significant amount of obstacles in his life to become one of the greatest scientists in history. From birth, he had to fight for his life after being born prematurely. Then, he had to live out his childhood without a father and with a mother who left him behind to marry a reverend. And in his career, he had to overcome the criticism of his scientific peers. Nevertheless, Newton, as one of his contemporaries duly noted: *"was never sensible to any passion, was not subject to the common frailties of mankind, nor had any commerce with women—a circumstance which was assured me by the physician and surgeon who attended him in his last moments,"* which was not meant to be a compliment necessarily, but is a testament to the direction in which Newton's mind was focused on. Newton realized, much like Socrates, that the amount of information out there in the world is nearly infinite. Due to this fact, Newton was always looking for new discoveries to be made, despite constantly discovering and quantifying new aspects of the world, aspects that were already there already in plain sight. Oftentimes we forget that there are facets of our life that are right in front of our faces waiting to be discovered. We end this chapter with some intriguing words of his, which show the number one trait that all scientists have to this day. Pure curiosity about how the world works.

> *"What we know is a drop, what we don't know is an ocean."*

> *"Gravity explains the motions of the planets, but it cannot explain who sets the planets in motion."*

> *"Truth is ever to be found in the simplicity, and not in the multiplicity and confusion of things."*

> *"To myself I am only a child playing on the beach, while vast oceans of truth lie undiscovered before me"*

CHAPTER 14

Albert Einstein

(1879 – 1955)

Theoretical Physicist – Theory of Relativity, $E = MC^2$

"Strive not to be a success, but rather to be of value."

-   *Albert Einstein*

School Years

It is not often that your name becomes a synonymous noun for a smart person. Unless you're Albert Einstein, then your name is synonymous with a smart person, and for good reason. Einstein was one of the most brilliant minds in history. From an early age, Einstein exhibited a high proclivity for math and physics. For example, while Einstein was attending school in his youth, 16-year-old Einstein took the entrance exam to the Federal Polytechnic School in Zurich, where he performed abnormally well on the math and physics portions of the test but failed the overall test due to his lack of knowledge on other subjects he was supposed to have studied in school. Nevertheless, Einstein impressed one of the heads of the Zurich school and was admitted anyway, despite failing the entrance exam. The admittance marked the end of Einstein's fight with early education, which was something he despised from the beginning of his academic career. Einstein's reasoning for hating school was a killer of creativity due to its inherent regimental structure. At one point, Einstein forged a doctor's note to get him out of school so he could join his family while they were moving to Italy.

Even though he had gone to Italy to ditch school, he wrote an entire essay on "The the Investigation of the State of the Ether in a Magnetic Field", which is not what most 15-year-olds do when they get out of school. But Einstein was not like most kids, regardless of his age. By the time he was 12, Einstein had taught himself algebra, geometry, and the Pythagorean Theorem.

Which were subjects he was supposed to learn a few years down the road.

When he was 13, a tutor of Einstein observed that: *"At the time he was still a child, only thirteen years old, yet Kant's works, incomprehensible to ordinary mortals, seemed to be clear to him."* (As someone who has read old works of philosophy, I can corroborate this statement). Besides his tutor, there were other teachers who were not only baffled by Einstein's intelligence but usurped from their master-to-student relationship, particularly in the realm of mathematics. When Einstein was just 12 years old, his tutor, Max Talmud, was helping Einstein learn geometry, but before he could actually help him, *"[Einstein] had worked through the whole book. He thereupon devoted himself to higher mathematics... Soon the flight of his mathematical genius was so high I could not follow."*

Even at that age, Einstein was a genius. But by the time he graduated from the Zurich school very few people knew him. The bushy mustache resting under those droopy eyes stands in contrast to the mane of wild, mad scientist hair on top. This is the iconic image we all know and love. However, the vast majority of people in Germany had no idea who Einstein was. Even the people who made up the mathematics community in Germany were not well acquainted with Einstein, with most of them considering him a newcomer, which he was.

Revolutionary Ideas

Einstein's first step towards becoming the icon he is

today was through 4 scientific and mathematical papers that he released in 1905, the same year he earned his Ph.D. Prior to the release of his four papers, Einstein had worked a pencil pusher job at a patent office to make ends meet. However, once the physics community read his papers, specifically the mass-energy equivalence, he was given a teaching position and inducted into their small community of geniuses, who, upon extracting Einstein from the patent office and giving him a spot amongst themselves, had no idea what this upstart would accomplish over the next few decades, and what others would do with his revolutionary ideas.

For example, the paper that Einstein wrote about mass-energy equivalence includes the extremely famous math equation $E = MC^2$, and this helped to jump-start the nuclear weapons movement in the 30s, 40s, and 50s. Generally speaking, Einstein is more commonly associated with his theory of relativity, which is an equation that is also based on $E=MC^2$ and helped introduce concepts like space-time, the origins, and purpose of black holes, and many other cosmological phenomena that are common knowledge today, thanks to the brilliance of Einstein. The theory also helped future physicists develop the Big Bang Theory, which offered a scientific explanation for the origins of the entire universe, a groundbreaking discovery that altered the way in which humans saw everything from religion to our purpose for existence. However, in modern history, Einstein's theories on atomic energy had a much more, we'll say, empirical effect. (Despite only two atomic bombs being dropped intentionally on an urban population).

Throughout his career as a scientist and mathematician, Einstein made many great discoveries that helped shape modern history. He also experienced many setbacks and adversities on his journey to becoming the most famous scientist of all time. But perhaps his biggest triumph was in 1919 when everything he worked for and believed in regarding gravity and his theory of general relativity hung in the balance.

The 1919 Solar Eclipse

WW1 had just ended, and the main empires in Europe had fallen. A revolution was happening, and Einstein was forbidden to travel outside of Germany. Enter Arthur Stanley Eddington. An astronomer interested in Einstein's theory due to its wide-ranging implications for cosmology and astrophysics, Eddington took on the task of proving it. By harnessing an image of a total solar eclipse, the deflection, or bending, of light by the Sun's gravity could be measured. This test was critical in the world of science because Einstein's theory predicted a deflection precisely twice the value obtained using Isaac Newton's law of universal gravitation. The needed eclipse was coming on May 29th, 1919, and the location was the island of Príncipe off the coast of West Africa.

Astronomers had tried and failed to capture an image of a solar eclipse in 1914 due to cloudy weather.

To make matters worse, William W Campbell, a US astronomer, now had calculations and proof that Newton's theory was more accurate than Einstein's, and he was about to announce it to the Royal Astronomical Society in London, where all the top world scientists and experts meet. This was a crucial moment in history.

Eddington set off on his journey to the island and spent 10 weeks at sea before finally arriving. You would think the hard part of the job was done, but this was just the beginning. He then had to hack his way through this African jungle where poisonous snakes lay everywhere, and malaria was rampant. He then had to find a suitable location and build a telescope with the help of his team.

When the fateful day arrived, Eddington and his team faced terrible weather. Thunderstorms rolled in. Clouds obscured the sun all day. Eddington was devastated. Distraught. Suddenly, a gap in the clouds appeared, and he saw a black moon. He knew this was the moment, and he had to begin taking photos right then! He started aligning the mirrors and other equipment and began inserting photographic plates over and over, hoping that some of the plates captured the image they needed. There was no time for finesse and double-checking exposure and accuracy. He said he was operating on blind faith, taking as many images as he could in the short time frame he had. Most of the images were worthless, but the last few plates had something of note. He was so excited that he began doing measurements in the jungle but knew it would be months before he could get back to London and work through the calculations correctly. There was still a long way to go.

When he eventually arrived back in London, he attended a meeting with the Royal Astronomical Society, where he announced that he hadn't finished the measurements yet, but the preliminary findings showed Einstein could be right. William Campbell then urgently faxed the US authorities and media to delay publishing Einstein's results as wrong.

Finally, a couple of months later, on November 6th, 1911, Eddington finalized his results and announced them to the Royal Astronomical Society in London, with the world watching. A portrait of Isaac Newton was overlooking the ceremony. Eddington began the meeting by pointing at the portrait of Newton, the founder of the Royal Society, saying;

'forgive us, Sir Isaac Newton, your universe has been overturned.'

He explains that Einstein's theory of relativity has been verified by the images of the solar eclipse and calculations taken from them. The public interest generated by this was tremendous, and Einstein was shot into superstardom instantly. A truly inspirational story and an iconic moment in history.

Although this chapter is about Einstein, Without Eddington, relativity would have gone unproven, and Einstein would have never become the icon of genius. Eddington called this the greatest moment of his life: *"I knew that Einstein's theory had stood the test and the new outlook of scientific thought must prevail."*

Eddington was Einstein's most crucial ally, though they did not meet until years after the war's end. Their collaboration was essential not only to the birth of modern physics but to the survival of science as an international community through the darkest days of World War One.

To end this chapter, I want to remind you that although Einstein was extremely knowledgeable, it must be remembered that he valued imagination over knowledge. That is where many feel his genius came from.

Here are some final quotes on his take on the importance of imagination:

> *"I am enough of an artist to draw freely upon my imagination. Imagination is more important than knowledge. Knowledge is limited. Imagination encircles the world."*

> *"Logic will get you from A to Z; imagination will get you everywhere."*

> *"I have no special talents. I am only passionately curious."*

CHAPTER 15

Leonardo Da Vinci

(1452 - 1519)

Italian Artist and Polymath of the High Renaissance

"The human foot is a masterpiece of engineering and a work of art."

- Leonardo Da Vinci

Da Vinci is famous for many great accomplishments. But most people have no idea that one of the most successful polymaths in history used to dissect corpses. For science, of course. Leonardo was trying to study the human body and understand its intricacies. For what though? Da Vinci already had success in painting, engineering, and dozens of other sciences. And he wasn't a doctor. So why would someone who's already pretty busy painting masterpieces take the time to study human anatomy?

Though there have been brilliant brains throughout history, his seemed to function on a different level. Da Vinci was not necessarily more intelligent than other Renaissance figures. However, it was the scope that his intelligence consumed that made his brain so special. His mind was like no other in history. It created unique pieces like the Mona Lisa and designed technology that wasn't even possible to invent during his lifetime. And just like his designs, Da Vinci's origins were unorthodox.

Early Life

Though his father was a high-standing notary, Da Vinci did not receive the life of a wealthy Italian child. The year was 1452, and the day was April 15th when Da Vinci was born to parents who were not married to each other. According to oral history, Da Vinci's mother birthed him in a small town that would not attract too much attention to his controversial birth. Historians believe that it's also very plausible that he was born in his father's house outside Florence. The most fascinating aspect of Da Vinci's birth details, besides his bizarre first memory that we'll get into later, is how long his father's name was Ser Piero d'Antonio di Ser Piero di Ser Guido da Vinci. At least he's got plenty of good nickname options.

Given the vast majority of mythology surrounding the documentation of Da Vinci's childhood, it is difficult to separate fact from fantasy, and thus is not deemed reliable.

His historical life really began after his rudimentary education, when Da Vinci joined the studio of Andrea Del Verrocchio at 14. By the time Da Vinci hit 17, he was an official apprentice to the studio. He began collaborating with Verrocchio on various art projects until, according to legend, Da Vinci's version of The Baptism of Christ blew his own project out of the water, causing the master to allegedly quit painting forever.

Another amusing childhood story (also to be taken with a grain of salt) entails young Da Vinci being hired by a peasant to draw an image on the client's homemade shield. His father, San Piero, saw the design Leonardo went with and decided not to give it to his peasant friend. The image was of Medusa and was deemed so terrifying by San Piero that he bought his friend a whole new shield as compensation. This story, whether true or not, is meant to show the great vivid skill Da Vinci had throughout his career.

Florence Art Industry

Despite being younger than most of his contemporaries, Da Vinci rose to prominence in the Florence art industry. Like so many other Italian Renaissance painters, he began his career by being commissioned by someone with lots of money to create portraits of Christian figures. Eventually, Da Vinci started a working relationship with the Medici family. In 1482, the Medicis sent Da Vinci to Milan, initially for political purposes, though he eventually took commissions for a few different religious pieces. You might have heard of one called the Last Supper, which Da Vinci painted for a monastery in 1496, and Dan Brown turned into a conspiracy theory in his controversial 2003 novel the Da Vinci Code. The book alleges that Jesus was married to Mary Magdalene and had a child with her. He argues, or his character Teabing argues, that there are symbols hidden in the painting Da Vinci intentionally left behind to tell others that Jesus was married to Mary Magdeline. The theories in the book, however, have no historical merit. However, scholars are still debating the context behind the odd structure of the disciples surrounding Jesus to this day. Overall, the painting is a reminder of Da Vinci's other great love that he often integrated into his art, mechanical engineering.

Human Anatomy

In a letter he wrote to a friend, Da Vinci describes himself as an engineer full of ideas on how to improve architecture and weapons (Da Vinci was obsessed with making literal killing machines, but we'll get to that later), only mentioning that he could also paint as if it was his side hustle. He made it clear to his friend and top patron, the Duke of Milan, that his main point of focus was on engineering. Da Vinci's love for more technical sciences can be seen in the well-balanced composition of his paintings. There is always some sort of geometric or symmetrical structure in the character position and background positioning in almost all of Da Vinci's paintings. He was perhaps the most effective user of the pyramid structure, where the three main subjects are each positioned at the three points of a triangle.

Da Vinci's obsession with human anatomy also contributed to the unique ways he positioned his subjects. They're often pleasing to the eye, but none is quite as eye-catching as Da Vinci's Saint John the Baptist. To our modern eyes, the way Saint John is pointing upward with his elbow in partial flexion, it looks like he's telling us, "up yours." If you gain some religious context, however, you'll know that the odd positioning of John the Baptist's arm is because the Saint is supposed to be pointing up toward heaven, signifying that God is the only true avenue to salvation. This depiction of Saint John the Baptist is a very dark, eerie version of the well-known saint. Da Vinci achieved this aesthetic using his pioneering painting technique called chiaroscuro, in which:

> *"A painter should begin every canvas with a wash of black, because all things in nature are dark except where exposed by the light."*

Leonardo used his masterful understanding of how to use colors to create shadows and depth, which made his pieces look alive. One great example is Da Vinci's most famous piece, the Mona Lisa, which combines his knowledge of anatomy and mastery of depth to create a portrait that people are still trying to figure out to this day.

By manipulating the shadows around her eyes and mouth, no viewer can decide if she is smiling or not. Given Da Vinci's intense studying of the anatomy of facial expressions, the ambiguity and complexity of his subject's inward emotions make a lot of sense. Leonardo Da Vinci didn't just want to understand everything. He needed to understand everything. He even says so himself:

> *"The noblest pleasure is the joy of understanding."*

Through his addiction to context, Da Vinci was able to integrate elements of various disciplines into his many creative ventures, including his engineering projects and ideas. Though he is perhaps best known for his art (thanks to Dan Brown and the guy who stole the Mona Lisa), Da Vinci was also a great inventor and engineer.

In the same way, he integrated science into arts, Da Vinci, in turn, combined his scientific studies with art. His number one method for analyzing the human body, designing machines and buildings, documenting animals, fossils, and many other subjects was to meticulously draw them out on paper. In other words, Da Vinci used art to gain the understanding he desperately craved. Or

as he put it:

> *"The painter who is familiar with the nature of the sinews, muscles, and tendons, will know very well, in giving movement to a limb, how many and which sinews cause it; and which muscle, by swelling, causes the contraction of that sinew; and which sinews, expanded into the thinnest cartilage, surround and support the said muscle."*

Engineering Designs

Da Vinci combined his eclectic knowledge to construct a legacy that spans dozens of disciplines, leaving us with a plethora of crazy inventions to examine today. My personal favorite is the tank. Many of Da Vinci's engineering sketches inspired future engineers and scientists, but the tank was not of those sketches. The armored vehicle was never constructed in Da Vinci's time simply because, like many of his other ideas, the concept was impractical for actual use. Engineers today deem the tank too heavy and immobile to be effective on a battlefield. Here is a brief description of the tank itself: The top was an umbrella-shaped covering made of wood and armored by an outer shell of metal. Under the round covering was a round room where two large cranks moved the wheels underneath, surrounded by several canons aimed outwards that fully circumvented the entire circle.

On paper, it sounds like an indestructible killing machine—cannonballs firing in every direction while the angled roof deflects projectiles—but the tank would actually be more of a liability than a useful weapon.

For starters, with all the men and heavy cannon equipment inside, the vehicle would be too heavy to move. And if it could move, its size and shape would make the tank nearly impossible to maneuver efficiently, meaning that the so-called tank is more of a cool mini fortress than an actual vehicle. However, the concept is cool and certainly original, even if Da Vinci copied the design from turtles.

Contrary to the tank's unsuccessful design, Da Vinci helped engineer several innovative technologies for his patrons. Such as a system to divert water from the nearby Arno River to prevent flooding. Da Vinci also pioneered the study of anatomy by devising the now-common method of showing the insides of the human body through the explosion method. This is when the organs and internal tissues are exposed while still being depicted within their location in the body, allowing today's students a first-hand examination of the intricacies of the human body without having to cut someone open like a Christmas ham.

First Memory and Fascination of Flight

Leonardo was fascinated by the phenomenon of flight, producing many studies on the flight of birds, including his c. 1505 Codex on the Flight of Birds, as well as drawing plans for several flying machines, such as a helicopter and a light hang glider. Most were impractical, like his aerial screw helicopter design that could not provide lift. However, the hang glider has since been successfully constructed and demonstrated.

This obsession with flight stems back from a vivid dream or first memory he had as a child. In this memory, Leonardo is in his cradle in a field. He remembers a kite flying above him, making ever-narrowing circles until it plunged from the sky and dropped on top of him. The bird did not scratch Leonardo with its claws or peck him with its beak. It simply flapped its wings and tried to open the boy's mouth with its forked tail. When Leonardo's mouth was opened in this way, the kite struck his lips and his tongue with its tail. It is something Da Vinci had never forgotten, and now that he was studying the mathematical laws that had to do with a bird's flight, that kite seemed to him to have been some kind of messenger telling him his future destiny.

All of these great accomplishments add up to the life of a great man who used his passion for learning and art to change the world. When Da Vinci died in 1519 at the age of 67, the peninsula of Italy mourned the end of a genius. It makes one think, how can I possibly be like Da Vinci? Out of all these great figures, his incredible array of talent and intellect seems unattainable. As it so happens, however, Da Vinci is probably the easiest of the historical figures to emulate. So to end this chapter, I'm going to let Leonardo remind us that:

"Learning never exhausts the mind."

CHAPTER 16

Cleopatra
(69 BC – 30 BC)

Queen of the Ptolemaic Kingdom of Egypt

"There was sweetness also in the tones of her voice; and her tongue, like an instrument of many strings, she could readily turn to whatever language she pleased..."

- *Plutarch*

Cleopatra, in the minds of modern-day pop culture absorbers, is the quintessential Egyptian queen. She conjures up fantastic images of braided wigs, amulets, lavish rides on the Nile, and being the seductive Egyptian woman in every adaptation of her life story. It might shock you, maybe even make you gasp, to know that the famed Egyptian queen was not actually Egyptian at all. She was as Greek as a gyro smothered in fresh tzatziki sauce.

There are many misconceptions of Cleopatra perpetuated by storytellers like Shakespeare and the dozens of Hollywood adaptations. In essence, Cleopatra's legacy is much more than misconstrued by recent media portrayals. It is clouded. That inevitably helped create the image of her that we have today. The key is to blow the clouds away and try to get the best glimpse possible at the real Cleopatra.

The Cleopatra who was a major player in the battle for Roman Empire supremacy, perhaps having a hand in taking down the republic that preceded the now-famous empire. The Cleopatra that was neither the gorgeous Egyptian seductress nor was she the homely Machiavellian maniac that others claim, who, in truth, was a bit of both. As with most cases in history, the most accurate portrait is never black or white, and Cleo is no exception (I hope she's okay with me calling her that.)

The first thing you need to know about Cleopatra is that she was more of a politician than a queen. Plutarch wrote most of the descriptions we have of Cleopatra, though historians, as they should, doubt the reliability of his documentation. Nevertheless, his accounts can still give us a pretty accurate account of Cleopatra. Here is his portrait of Cleo the politician:

> *"Judging by the proofs which she had had before this of the effect of her beauty upon Gaius (Julius) Caesar and Gnaeus the son of Pompey, she had hopes that she would more easily bring Antony to her feet. For Caesar and Pompey had known her when she was still a girl and inexperienced in affairs, but she was going to visit Antony at the very time when women have the most brilliant beauty and are at the acme of intellectual power"*

Plutarch makes her sound pretty ruthless and, as many fans of Shakespeare would have it, a Machiavellian seductress, which was pretty truthful given her past, specifically before she tried to win the affections of Mark Antony.

Heritage

The second thing you need to know about Cleopatra is how Greek she was and all how much that had to do with her being a politician. Cleopatra was born into a dynasty of Greek kings known as the Ptolemys (the P is like films before 1927, silent). They were born from one of the fragments of Alexander the Great's short-lived empire. After he died, Alexander's generals carved up his empire into chunks that included Egypt, which Ptolemy I took as his share, declaring himself the new pharaoh in the process. This all happened around 300 BCE. By the time Cleopatra was born in 69 BCE. Her family was widespread and deformed by centuries of incestuous marriages. Which is one reason modern-day scholars dispute Cleo's famed beauty. If you're wondering what I'm talking about, just look up the 'Habsburg Jaw,' and you'll understand why Cleopatra possibly wasn't the reddest apple in the barrel.

Cleopatra was one of the senior members of the family, eventually becoming queen of the dynasty. Her ascension began with the death of her brother Ptolemy XIII, who was her co-ruler for only a couple of years at the most, due to Cleopatra rejecting his marriage proposal. If your jaw just dropped, you'd be in the minority in Ptolemaic Egypt. Sibling marriages were a common practice that the Ptolemy family adopted from the ancient pharaohs, meaning that, according to dynasty tradition, Cleopatra's rejection was probably a sign of non-co-operation, beyond just romance. Marriage was political in those days, and when chroniclers recorded in a temple that Cleopatra had turned down Ptolemy XIII, she was essentially implying that half of their kingdom would not suffice.

Ascension to the Throne/Julius Caesar

From that point forward, Cleopatra had a rough ascension to the throne. Her brother Ptolemy XII proved to be a talented military man and defeated his sister, forcing Cleopatra to flee Alexandria, the capital of the Ptolemies, and hide in temporary exile in Thebes, a region in modern-day Greece. After some consolidation, Cleopatra returned to her home city with hopes of beating her brother and claiming the throne for herself. However, Cleo was caught in a stalemate until Julius Caesar showed up, and according to historical sources, was won over to Cleopatra's side by her powerful persuasion skills. And by persuasion, they mean sex. Not to be crude, but Julius Caesar had already obtained a well-known reputation for hooking up with royal women on his travels, and Cleopatra needed his support to win back her throne. Put another way; they were a perfect couple. At least for the time being.

Julius Caesar, through the power he held in Rome, helped Cleopatra navigate the complicated political situation left behind by Ptolemy XII. And after a series of tumultuous events, including a siege, and ending with her brother Ptolemy XIII drowning after a naval battle, he helped Cleopatra secure a marriage with her 12-year-old brother and, through their messed-up unity, stabilized the kingdom. Even though she was married to her little brother, Cleopatra still lived with Julius Caesar and ended up bearing the Roman conqueror's children. They are said to have been quite a romantic couple indeed, though the sappy stuff was probably embellished a tad by ancient historians, sort of like how modern tabloids and journalists fantasize about the love lives of celebrities. One historian, Suetonius, provides details about how Julius Caesar and Cleopatra took a pleasure cruise along the Nile. By all accounts, they seemed to be the ancient equivalent of a power couple, despite not being legally married. But if you know anything about ancient history, or Shakespeare for that matter, then you probably know what is going to happen next.

Unbeknownst to Cleopatra, her relationship with Julius Caesar would bring about her eventual downfall. But not before Caesar brought himself down. I probably don't have to tell you about the Ides of March, only that the event had a major butterfly effect on Cleopatra, besides the probable heartbreak she was feeling. Cleopatra was now left without a political protector. Julius Caesar was one of the most powerful men on earth, and most likely, if the tabloid historians are correct, very much in love with her. But now the Roman republic was fragmented, divided up between two sides, one led by Mark Antony, while the other was led by Caesar's nephew Octavian (soon to be Caesar Augustus), neither of whom Cleopatra had any leverage, like love, over. And for the past decade, Rome had its eye on Ptolemaic Egypt, with one senator vigorously trying to pass a bill that would make the government annex Cleopatra's home into Roman hands. The stakes were high for Cleopatra and her family. Something needed to be done.

Fortunately, Cleopatra was already quite familiar with ruthless political moves. You don't become the most powerful woman in the world at a sausage party by being Sally goody two shoes. In the famous Shakespeare play Antony and Cleopatra, the queen says:

> *"Give me my robe, put on my crown; I have*
> *Immortal longings in me: now no more*
> *The juice of Egypt's grape shall moist this*
> *lip"*

Cleopatra and Mark Antony both needed allies. Cleo needed protection from Rome, while Mark Antony needed a place to stay and build up his army. Rome was in a civil war, a fight between two men who had claims to the rulership of the now newly-christened empire. And thanks to ancient writers, Shakespeare, and Hollywood directors from the 20s and 60s, almost everyone over 50 is familiar with the story of Antony and Cleopatra.

They first met when Cleopatra invited him to stay with her in Egypt and allowed Antony to live with her in her luxurious Alexandrian palace, and it was not long before Antony fully moved in with Cleopatra, residing within the relatively safe and extremely fancy confines of her capital city.

Although most writers depicted the couple in a fiery romance, their relationship was cultivated primarily for political advantages. By most accounts, Antony was the most powerful man in Rome (despite spending none of this period in the city) while Cleopatra was the monarch in charge of the most powerful kingdom around the

Mediterranean not occupied by the Romans. Their union made a lot of sense from a political strategy perspective. They both wanted the other's resources and prestige, so they sealed the deal with two children, which they both proudly claimed as their own.

The literal power couple spent their remaining time together in Egypt on Cleopatra's riverboat, the ancient equivalent of a souped-up Viking river cruise on the Nile, before Antony left to go on a military campaign around the Mediterranean. Cleopatra gave him 200 ships which sent him off well-armed, and a spy to keep watch on Antony.

Antony would not return for some time, and when he did, the powerful Roman came back with a new wife and two other children that were not Cleopatra's. From there, they more or less broke up but still reaped the benefits of their powerful union until everything fell apart in epic proportions.

Downfall and Death
Shit really hit the fan when Cleopatra's escape fleet was destroyed. She had initially planned to escape Egypt to recuperate and perhaps find a way to reclaim her kingdom from Octavian. But before she could depart, a jealous rival burned the fleet, leaving Cleopatra isolated, waiting for Octavian to show up on her palace doorstep. And eventually, he did. But not before defeating Cleopatra's husband (or baby daddy, depending on your perspective) in a final battle for the supremacy of Rome. In the aftermath of the battle, Antony fell on his own

sword, destroying any hope Cleopatra had of preserving her kingdom from Octavian, who landed in Egypt not long after.

The new emperor of Rome captured Cleopatra's palace and three children. With no escape in sight and the thought of losing her kingdom and being the last monarch in the dynasty, the Ptolemaic queen committed suicide.

Though her end was tragic, Cleopatra nevertheless led an incredible and inspiring life. She was one of the most important political figures in the powerful and chaotic world of the ancient Mediterranean. All while having a uterus, an impressive accomplishment 2,000 years ago. Overall, Cleopatra shows us what's possible if we're willing to do whatever it takes to achieve our goals, even if it means saying no to our brother's marriage proposal.

Here are some of her most famous quotes:

"Fool! Don't you see now that I could have poisoned you a hundred times had I been able to live without you."

"I will not be triumphed over"

"I had come to Rome in chains but I would leave a queen'

CHAPTER 17

Socrates

(470 BCE – 399 BCE)

Ancient Greek Philosopher

"I know that I know nothing"

- *Socrates*

Imagine going about your day, browsing the grocery store, or filling your car up with gas. Then out of nowhere, a random guy with a bushy beard asks you why you choose gas over electric. Besides being mildly annoyed you give him a basic answer, to which the bearded man immediately follows up with another question, and another...and another. Until you start developing a strong desire to plunge your fist into that big bushy beard.

This was, according to Plato's 'Dialogues,' how Socrates developed his now-famous Socratic Method. By questioning average everyday people's morals and ethical beliefs, and inspiring a new school of thought, that in turn inspired science and almost every other branch of philosophical thought in the western hemisphere. Hence the dogma, 'question everything.'

Ironically, Socrates' life is an enigma that has been thoroughly questioned by historians for millennia. His followers, primarily Plato, wrote down some of Socrates' life details and teachings. In addition to Plato's writings, several plays were written about him as well, mostly due to the great dramatic quality of his death, which we'll get to in a minute.

Early Life

Let's start at the beginning. Socrates was born in the western philosophical epicenter of Athens in 470 BCE. From his birth, we don't know a whole lot about the life of Socrates. And what we do know was not written by Socrates himself. Because the OG philosopher never created his own works like other thinkers did in Ancient Athens. This lack of literature is in part due to Socrates's overall view of himself and how rigorously he followed his own teachings. Despite him preaching wisdom, Socrates did not believe that he himself was wise (as the quote 'I know that I know nothing' indicates). Since Socrates did not think he had wisdom to offer the Ancient Athenians, he wrote nothing down.

Meaning that Socrates' life story is a Wikipedia page but with way more authors. Most historians mainly draw from the works by Plato who treat Socrates as a character in a philosophical story, and the more historical works by Xenophon. These sources, however, should be considered with caution. Historians do not doubt the existence of Socrates, or the overall message that Socrates was trying to convey to the people of Athens. For example, some scholars believe that the Socrates portrayed by Plato is a slightly idealized or romantic version of Socrates. This is probably true given Plato's habit of being a political idealist. However, the quotes and teachings from Plato's works about or featuring Socrates can still be trusted. In the same way Christians trust the Gospels, lovers of philosophy can trust the quotes provided by Plato. At least historians believe so.

Nevertheless, the ironic lack of words is nevertheless a testament to his genius. Before he became a genius, however, Socrates lived a relatively normal 'Hellenistic' life. This includes military service and participating in the polis. According to Plato,

Socrates was a war hero in the Peloponnesian War (a massive conflict fought between the city-states Sparta and Athens) and went on to use his status to participate in a few other political events before becoming a fully committed philosopher.

Socrates was also a fan of wrestling, though he mainly used the Greek sport for socializing and physical exercise, something many Greeks did in Athens as part of the individualistic Hellenized mindset. When he wasn't wrestling with his buddies and debating in the agora, Socrates was with his wife Xanthippe, and their three sons. Not much is known about Socrates' family life, with most of the attention being focused on his philosophical teachings. His wife, for instance, is only known to have had a fiery temper. This is why he might have spent so much time at the agora, asking people unwanted questions in the streets.

As mentioned before in the gas station story, Socrates was a moralist and ethically focused thinker and critic. Emphasis on the word critic. His many questions, including the kinds that were asked to strangers just going about their day, were known to stir up trouble on the streets of Ancient Athens.

With comments like this:

> *"A system of morality which is based on relative emotional values is a mere illusion, a thoroughly vulgar conception which has nothing sound in it and nothing true."*

Even today that quote might ruffle some self-righteous feathers. See, back then a philosopher spoke and or debated publicly in the Agora with other philosophers. Thinkers like Socrates had loyal followers, and schools, and were well-known in the community. Similar to how we have public intellectuals today or famous religious figures. But instead of preaching encouraging sermons or scientific theories, Socrates decided to aim his word arrows right at the worst people possible—the ones in charge of everything. This quote here summarizes his views on the ethics of politicians:

> *"I was really too honest a man to be a politician and live."*

Although we don't know exactly what Socrates said about politicians of the day, we can be certain he must have said something like this. Since Athens was a democracy, the opinion of the people was an important asset to the wealthy powerful politicians of the day. According to Socrates' many biographers, a major catalyst that contributed to his death was the philosopher's harsh criticisms of the politicians of Ancient Athens. More specifically, however, his overall critiques of democracy itself, an institution that Athens held a lot of pride in.

Death

Some historians believe Socrates was killed due to other causes, like how annoying Socrates was. Plato refers to him as a gadfly, one of the peskiest and most bothersome bugs in Ancient Greece, always buzzing into people's business, just like Socrates. Recalling the gas station scene once again, it's not difficult to imagine, or at least entertain the idea of harming an unasked-for moral policeman. Either way, some Athenians became fed up with Socrates and put him on trial for corrupting the youth to denounce their belief in the gods. A charge that the court found him guilty of. Historians believe given the political instability of Athens (they had just lost the Peloponnesian wars and were being fought over by two opposing powers), that the trial was rigged to get rid of Socrates. Perhaps due to his apparent disdain for democracy and iconoclastic praise of Sparta, the politicians who supported democracy wanted the influential philosopher out of the way.

You might've heard of the trial and execution of Socrates, but you probably didn't know that he was given a chance to escape. According to a later source, a few of Socrates' dedicated students bribed the guards and planned to sneak him out of the city under the cover of night. However, Socrates refused to leave, and also cost his students a lot of wasted bribe money. The reason Socrates said no to escaping his execution is perhaps the most romantic part of his legend. Socrates had been sentenced to poisoning via oral ingestion of hemlock, a lethal plant that was broken down into a drink and force-fed to the charged criminal when the time came. In a show of defiance, dedication, and virtue, Socrates ingested the poison himself in 399 BCE—

dying shortly after from what most historians technically deem a suicide. He died on his accord as a statement to the merit of his own philosophy; what many call the Socratic Method.

His followers mostly wrote his philosophical debates with people on issues of morality and ethics. However, its Socrates' quotes of wisdom that attains him the most admiration today. Particularly from the now popular Stoic movement—a philosophy being used in fragments by thought leaders such as psychologist Jordan Peterson and social media guru Gary Vaynerchuk.

A famous quote attributed to him is very stoic in that it focuses on self-improvement and self-reflection, both were important topics for Socrates:

"An unexamined life is not worth living."

It is through Socrates' unique and simple path to wisdom that you can take inspiration. In fact, none of the inspirational stories in this book matter much if you don't learn wisdom. Which is a combination of the two things, according to the overall message from Socrates. Admit that you know nothing, but always strive for more knowledge. Socrates himself says:

"True wisdom comes to each of us when we realize how little we understand about life, ourselves, and the world around us."

He follows up with this bit about true wisdom:

"Wisdom begins in wonder."

This wonder Socrates talks about can be construed as curiosity. Recognizing that you don't know anything and must constantly be seeking new knowledge is Socrates' message for us. Knowledge about the world and knowledge about ourselves. Which, especially in times of political and cultural division, can be beneficial for helping us understand each other and be more compassionate people.

However, Socrates wasn't just all talk. Another big inspiration chunk you can draw from the life of Socrates is the conviction he held till the end, the very end in fact. Socrates was willing to die for what he believed in and do the killing himself just to make a point. I'm not saying you should make yourself a martyr, but we could all stand up for our beliefs a little more as Socrates did. And question things every now and then just to be sure we are on the right moral path.

I'll leave you with some final Socrates quotes:

"Be kind, for everyone you meet is fighting a hard battle."

"Strong minds discuss ideas, average minds discuss events, weak minds discuss people."

"By all means marry; if you get a good wife, you'll become happy; if you get a bad one, you'll become a philosopher."

"He who is not contented with what he has, would not be contented with what he would like to have."

"The secret of happiness, you see, is not found in seeking more, but in developing the capacity to enjoy less."

CHAPTER 18

Wolfgang Amadeus Mozart

(1756 – 1791)

Music Composer

"They probably think because I am so small and young, nothing of greatness and class can come out of me; but they shall soon find out."

- *Wolfgang Amadeus Mozart*

"A goodly number of high nobility was present: the Duchess Kickass, the Countess Pisshappy, also the Princess Smellshit with her two daughters, who are married to the two Princes of Mustbelly von Pigtail," was how Mozart described his clientele in Salzburg, his hometown in the now-defunct Holy Roman Empire. Mozart's time in Salzburg was the equivalent of a modern musician trying to make it in his hometown, meanwhile dreaming of the day they would make it big in L.A. or Nashville. For Mozart, his L.A. was the city of Vienna, the capital of Austria. Though he was finding success in the courts of Salzburg, Mozart dreamed of playing before the king, a dream he held since he was a child. A very young child.

Born in 1756, Mozart had only just graduated from being a toddler when he began his music composition career. As his older sister Nannerl recalls:

> *"He often spent much time at the clavier, picking out thirds, which he was ever striking, and his pleasure showed that it sounded good. ... In the fourth year of his age his father, for a game as it were, began to teach him a few minutes and pieces at the clavier. ... He could play it faultlessly and with the greatest delicacy, and keeping exactly in time. ... At the age of five, he was already composing little pieces, which he played to his father who wrote them down."*

Before most children learned to read or even spell their names, Mozart was composing music, a task reserved for a very minuscule portion of the music-loving population. However, Mozart seemed to have already mastered the art.

Child Prodigy

During his early years, and even when he aged into adulthood, Mozart was treated as a child prodigy. Mozart's father, and teacher, Leopold Mozart, upon realizing his son's precocious musical talent, gave up on his own composition attempts and instead sought to capitalize on its potential value to the avid music scene in Austria, which consisted almost entirely of wealthy aristocrats, the only Austrians who could afford to hire musicians or singers to perform in live concerts. Leopold gathered his two gifted children (Nanneri was also a talented musician in her own right) and embarked on a traveling classical music roadshow. Their show debuted in front of the Prince-elector Maximilian III, a very high honor to be bestowed upon children. Mozart was the age that most of us are when we learn what 2 x 8 is when he performed before royalty. The touring firmly cemented Mozart as a child prodigy, a label he would carry with him throughout his career, often with lamentation. When he became an adult performer, Mozart said that:

> *"What annoys me most is that these stupid Frenchmen think I am still just seven years old - because that was my age when they first saw me - (...) they treat me here like a*

beginner - except the musicians; they know better."

The musicians were correct. Mozart was only a prodigy until he became too old to be a prodigy, a fact the French seemed not to understand. Even today, Mozart is misunderstood. In his day, the majority of Austrians perceived him as we do today, a talented musician and composer who woke up one morning and became a master. However, Mozart knew his gift was no miraculous coincidence. One time a friend of Mozart's was "fixing his eyes on my fingers while I played to him, then said suddenly: *My God; I work at it till I sweat and yet get no success - while you, my friend, simply play at it!"* To which Mozart retorted,

"Yes, but I too had to work in order that I might be exempt from work now."

In other words, as Mozart put it more directly:

"It is a mistake to think that the practice of my art has become easy to me. I assure you, dear friend, no one has given so much care to the study of composition as I. There is scarcely a famous master in music whose works I have not frequently and diligently studied."

The fruit of all this diligent studying was an impressive musical career. Impressive in that Mozart became perhaps the greatest composer and performer in all of Austria. Despite dying in 1791 at the spry age of 35, Mozart created over 600 compositions, many of which changed classical music forever.

Salzburg and Vienna

It all began when Mozart began playing gigs in front of the so-called "Duchess Kickass" and "Princess Smellshit" in Salzburg. Even though he had found fruitful patronage with the Prince-Archbishop of Salzburg and wrote many of his most famous violin concertos, Mozart left his hometown for Paris in 1778. He tried to find work there, but the salaries and jobs the French were offering him did not meet Mozart's standards. Due to the lack of revenue coming in while abroad, Mozart accumulated a substantial amount of debt, a problem that would plague the composer throughout his life, despite him earning a substantial amount of money in his career, a career that did not truly take off until Mozart moved to the central European musical capital known as Vienna. After finding no employment worthy of his perceived skill level, Mozart returned from his time abroad and attempted to find employment in the court of the Holy Roman Emperor.

Mozart was coming off strong after a successful opera he'd written in Munich, prompting a patron of his, the aforementioned Archbishop, to summon his musician to attend the ascension celebrations for the newly crowned Emperor Joseph II. As Mozart wrote to his father in a letter, he knew by then that:

> *"My main goal right now is to meet the emperor in some agreeable fashion, I am absolutely determined he should get to know me. I would be so happy if I could whip through my opera for him and then play a fugue or two, for that's what he likes."*

Upon his arrival in Vienna, Mozart was met with the same subpar treatment he had received from patrons abroad, and from his longtime advocate, the Archbishop. Though he had desired Mozart to come to Vienna during the Emperor's ascension celebrations, the Archbishop had no intention of sharing his musical employee with anyone else. Before the Industrial Revolution kicked into high gear 100 years later, in the late 19th century, the aristocracy ruled Europe with a white-gloved fist. For a commoner like Mozart, the only avenue he had toward employment was obtaining a nobleman's patronage. And when Mozart refused to work for the Archbishop due to the high-ranking clergyman's restraints, the young composer lost his patron. With no one paying the bills, Mozart needed someone powerful to pay him to play and write music. Thanks to the Archbishop, ironically, Mozart positioned himself to attain the support of the ultimate white-gloved fist.

The Emperor eventually heard Mozart play and was inevitably impressed by the musician's playing ability, as well as his talent for composing concertos and operas. While under the employment (or should I say part-time employment) of the Emperor, Mozart earned less than half the salary he took home in Salzburg.

Nevertheless, Mozart seemed to be quite happy living out his dream in Vienna. The small salary afforded him the opportunity to chase other ventures besides the wasteful ball music Emperor Joseph hired him to write and play. One particular venture Mozart branched out to with a raucous pace was opera. He once exclaimed in a letter;

> *"I have an inexpressible desire to write an opera again; it would make me so happy because it gives me something to compose which is my real joy and passion."*

Mozart's passion proved well-founded. The composer created some of the most innovative and iconic operas in history. Then Mozart suddenly stopped writing operas. In fact, his overall output slowed significantly. During Mozart's later years, he fell into a dry spell, in part due to depression, which led him to make deleterious decisions.

In the end, the majority of Mozart's income was derived from the Emperor's salary. Mozart also lacked the opportunity to quit his gig with Joseph II since the

Holy Roman Emperor ostensibly never gave his composer the option. These conditions caused Mozart to beg for loans from his wealthy friends and fall into a deep depression.

But despite all of this turmoil, Mozart continued composing music; even in his darkest hour, Mozart adhered to the chip on his shoulder. His whole life, he had something to prove to the world and worked harder than any other composer of his time to become the best of the best. Young composers, such as the then-unknown Ludwig Von Beethoven (see series 2), all wanted to absorb some of Mozart's genius. Though scholars are not sure if they ever met, Beethoven certainly wanted to. Of course, we, in the 21st century, cannot meet Mozart. However, we can study his life and perhaps borrow a fragment of Mozart's chip if we should ever be so lucky.

CHAPTER 19

Emmeline Pankhurst

(1858 – 1928)

English Political Activist for Women's Rights

"Trust in God - she will provide."

- Emmeline Pankhurst

When Emmeline was just 14, she attempted to join the Independent Labor Party. Being an idealistic young woman seeking to be a part of change, Emmeline felt that the part was the right place to be. But the Labor party declined her membership request because she happened to be of the opposite sex—serving as the Batman-like parental murderer that sparked one of the most influential suffrage careers in history. Only further exacerbated by the fact that she was born on Bastille Day, the day French Revolutionaries stormed the royal palace, a facet of herself she was very proud of. It seems as if everything in her life pointed to becoming an activist, and the Labor Party assured what cause Emmeline would take up.

The future suffragist was born on July 14th in the year, 1858, the middle of the Victorian era. It should be noted, however, that Emmeline was actually born on July 15th, a day after Bastille Day. It is she who claims that she was born on the 14th. Truly the attitude one needs to become a decent activist."

Political Roots
Emmeline grew up in the city of Manchester with her politically active family. In fact, her family's political activity, on both sides mind you, went back at least two generations. With activism literally in her DNA, Emmeline entered the world, and what a world it was.

Neither the UK nor the United States, the two most powerful countries in the world that allowed a certain degree of democratic representation, did not allow their women to vote. In fact, according to English law, a woman could not legally inherit a title from her father—a law that is still technically in place to this day.

Instead of passing judgment on this time period of ethical superiority (because I don't have that), I will let Emmeline take it from here. This is what Emmeline had to say about the time she lived in:

> *"Men make the moral code and they expect women to accept it. They have decided that it is entirely right and proper for men to fight for their liberties and their rights, but that it is not right and proper for women to fight for theirs."*

Essentially this is what Emmeline believed in and stood by her whole life. In this bio, we're going to go over all the things that Emmeline did to change the world she believed to be so messed up. Although Emmeline had a husband and children, she still devoted her life to this cause. And don't worry. There are more Emmeline quotes to come.

After being rejected from the Labor Party, an organization she hoped was going to lead the fight for women's suffrage, Emmeline had to look elsewhere to participate in the movement. One way she did this was by marrying a suffragist. In 1879 she married lawyer and activist Richard Pankhurst. Richard was known for his writings on women's suffrage and his support of it, a bold move for a guy back in those days.

Women's Franchise League

They went on to move to London and have five children, all while Emmeline fought for rights in different organizations until 1903. Before 1903, Emmeline joined the Women's Suffrage Society. The society, however, soon dissolved into different factions, leaving Emmeline without a clear place to go yet again. So she and a few other women founded an organization called the Women's Franchise League due to the organizations being too lax on their principles. Emmeline wanted to fight for all women to vote, whereas other groups were willing to compromise to just unmarried women because (get this) married woman's husbands could vote for them.

The first meeting for the WFL was held in Emmeline and Richard's home. They both participated in the founding of the organization, a husband-wife activist team #victoriancouplegoals.

It might surprise us today, through our model perceptions, but in the late 19th century, the WFL was considered by many to be a radical organization. Emmeline and Richard were pushing for legislation on subjects such as divorce and inheritance (remember the title law I talked about earlier). Of course, to us, the things that Emmeline fought so hard for are perfectly normal, certainly not radical. You'd be radical today if you supported married women losing their right to vote and probably get banned from Twitter in the process.

Due to the inherent lack of social media in Victorian England, society had other ways of dealing with radical views and vice versa. For example, Emmeline used abrasive tactics to attack her political opponents; her weapon of choice being the pen, of course. The articles she wrote attacking other suffrage movements were so radical and aggressive that many in the WFL abandoned ship. And you can't sail a large vessel without a crew (unless it's a ghost ship), so Emmeline's organization dissolved, and the fiery activist found herself at square one yet again.

On top of her failure to organize an effective activist group, Emmeline's family was falling on hard times. She and Richard took the family of 7 all around England, looking for something stable. At last, they found steady ground back in Manchester.

With more free time, Emmeline worked hard on becoming an influential suffragist and eventually put out work that solidified her as a legitimate member of the movement.

Fast forward to 1903, the important year I mentioned earlier, and we find Emmeline going back to her old methods of aggressive tactics. Except this time, everyone else is on the same page— that page being one of necessity. Or, as Emmeline put it:

> *"You have to make more noise than anybody else, you have to make yourself more obtrusive than anybody else, you have to fill all the papers more than anybody else, in fact you have to be there all the time and see that they do not show you under, if you are really going to get your reform realised."*

By 1903 the suffrage movement had gotten nowhere. Particularly with the current strategy the organizations were using in those days. In other words, the quiet simmer was quickly turning into a blistering gurgling boil, and Emmeline was one of the women turning up the stove.

Since her husband died in 1898, Emmeline lost not only her husband but a chunk of her influence in the suffrage community. Richard was a well-known writer of pro-suffrage content and Emmeline had actually been more or less riding his coattails for years. Towards the end of his life, however, Emmeline had made a name of her own. Now she had to carry on Richards's legacy and fulfill the law-making changes that they'd been fighting for all this time. It was a lot of pressure. Fortunately, Emmeline's kids had not fallen from the activist tree. One of her oldest children, Christabel, had actually gotten arrested in 1905 for spitting on a cop, although this happened 7 years after her father died. By 1905, almost everyone in the suffrage movement had the attitude of Christabel. Including Emmeline herself. Who, in 1908, along with her fellow suffragist leaders, really kicked things up a notch.

Turning Point

There were massive protests in Hyde Park that resulted in police using abusive force on the suffragists. This was a turning point for the movement as they subsequently became more militant. Emmeline was a big proponent of aggressive behavior. In fact, she voiced her approval of a group of suffragists who threw rocks at the windows of No. 10 Downing Street, making her stance on protesting pretty clear—achieve rights for women no matter the cost. Emmeline lived out this stance in her speeches and in her often brazen actions:

'I would rather be a rebel than a slave.''

Then going on to describe herself as:

"I am what you call a hooligan."

And a hooligan she was. Besides the many many speeches she conducted all around England and America, Emmeline participated in rowdy protests herself. Up to the four years before World War 1, Emmeline staged hunger strikes, where protesters would intentionally starve themselves until legislation was passed. In response, Emmeline and her fellow suffragettes were force-fed by police. Emmeline was imprisoned several times for her many protests, in which she would often continue her hunger-striking while in jail.

The police were so familiar by this point that any time they saw her on the street, they would harass her. To combat the police harassment, the suffragettes organized an all-female protection team trained in Brazilian Jiu-Jitsu to protect Emmeline (that part wasn't necessarily relevant to her life story, but I had to include it because it's really cool, you're welcome).

After years of intense protesting, imprisonment, and speaking, Emmeline halted her efforts in 1914. World War 1 became a much bigger priority for her and her family to help with. So, for the next 4 years, Emmeline helped her country get through the war but took up her old position as de-facto of the suffrage movement in the U.K. However, the fervor she possessed from 1910 to 1914 was slightly diminished. By the late 1920s, Emmeline could no longer protest like she used to and was primarily relegated to making speeches.

On June 14th, 1928, Emmeline Pankhurst died. She left the world as a conservative and in scandal, after her daughter, Sylvia, had a child out of wedlock (a huge no-no back in the 20s). She also left as an internationally famous advocate and activist for women's rights. However, her legacy at the time received mixed reviews. You could certainly accuse Emmeline Pankhurst of being a Machiavellian. And you're probably right in that assumption. The radical (in her time) suffragist did whatever it took to give women in England their legal right to vote. What it took was a lot of pain and struggle that needed someone strong to overcome it, and one of those people so happened to be Emmeline Pankhurst. She sold her house and lived a chaotic lifestyle of speeches, protests, and sporadic travel. Most of the time coming up just short of getting anything substantial done.

I'll leave you with a final quote of Emmeline's:

"Once they are aroused, once they are determined, nothing on earth and nothing in heaven will make women give way, it is impossible."

I don't doubt that for a second.

CHAPTER 20

Gautama Buddha
(563 BCE - 483 BCE) Or (480 BCE - 400 BCE)

Founder of Buddhism

"It is better to conquer yourself than to win a thousand battles. Then the victory is yours. It cannot be taken from you, not by angels or by demons, heaven or hell."

-   *Buddha*

We've all seen the iconic image of the Buddha. Whether it be in a Vietnamese nail salon or a glorious sculpture exhibited in a fine arts museum. Sometimes he's fat. Other times he's fit. Regardless of the image you see or connote, there is a historical Buddha. Much like Muhammad and Jesus, Buddha indeed has a historical version of himself, which simultaneously comes with a side of myth and shrines. And, much like the other religious founders, Buddha led a life that created the circumstances in which his teachings would be born. Thanks to these circumstances, our world is forever changed.

Origins

Born centuries before Muhammad and Jesus, Siddhartha Gautama entered the world around 480 BCE or 583 BCE, depending on whom you ask. His birthplace was the Shakya Republic, now the current location of Nepal. He wouldn't attain the title of Buddha until two centuries after his death. The title means *Enlightened One*. One aspect you need to understand about the biographical sources of Buddha is the progression toward deification. In other words, the farther away the source was from Buddha's lifetime, the more they portrayed him as a god-like figure. For example, the earlier depictions of Buddha don't include many of the attributes commonly associated with the divinity of Buddha. Attributes such as a painless birth and living hundreds of past lives. Personally, I'd believe the latter over the former. For historians, however, these biographies are like sifting for gold, or in this case, historical truths from a slew of posthumous myths. Most of you might have heard of the typical story of Buddha as a prince dealing with his famous existential crisis. After escaping his family's luxurious palace and seeing the suffering of the common folk, Buddha was exposed to the problems of the world. This realization led him to seek a path to escape suffering. Once he achieved enlightenment Buddha taught his followers the same path through some kind of monastic organization. This is the life story most of us are told. However, this version is based primarily on later sources that, as previously mentioned, attempt to deify the teacher they lovingly dubbed Buddha. While this was really nice of them, it makes his story very confusing. For that reason, when discussing the events of Buddha's life, we will focus on the earlier sources that tend not to make Buddha into a god because, unlike Christians or Muslims, not all Buddhists are on the deity train.

Upbringing

Buddha is an extremely complex figure. Regarding his childhood, the majority of sources do not provide a lot of details on his youth. You have to remember that Buddha was born almost three thousand years ago. That's a lot of time for things to get lost. The earliest sources do, however, give us modern folk some background on Buddha. For example, the story of Buddha being a prince isn't too far from the truth. According to early sources, Buddha was born into a family of wealthy rice farmers. It's much more likely that Buddha was an aristocrat than a prince, especially since historians know that the *Shakya* were governed by an oligarchy and not a monarchy. Nevertheless, Buddha did most likely grow up as the modern equivalent of a trust fund kid in Nepal. Sources use this as a great stepping stone to the famous renunciation. Earlier I mentioned that Buddha left his palace and became existentially altered after seeing the suffering of the common people. After he became enlightened, Buddha started a monastic organization where he taught his followers how to achieve the same spiritual awakening. While that story is probably embellished, the core of it is most likely true.

At some point in his life, Buddha truly did become discontent with his current life and sought something more meaningful. There have been many people who have felt this, but very few do anything about it. Buddha, on the other hand, actually pulled it off. He renounced his wealth and chose a life of poverty. The renunciation led Buddha to leave his family, which was devastating for them and probably difficult for Buddha as well as he began his journey, or, as it would later be called, the noble quest. On his quest, Buddha wandered through towns and cities as an ascetic wanderer, begging for what he needed and living off of whatever people would give him. As for the spiritual aspect of the journey, Buddha tried learning from various teachers who taught him their techniques for achieving a higher meaning. However, none of their lessons proved to meet exactly what Buddha was searching for. 'What exactly was Buddha looking for?' you're probably asking. The early Buddhist sources explain that during the Great Renunciation, Buddha was attempting to find a way to free himself of suffering, the same suffering he allegedly encountered outside the palace. Now you're probably asking if you're not familiar with the teachings of Buddhism, what does Buddha mean by suffering? The answer can be found in this swift quote attributed to Buddha that says:

"The root of suffering is attachment."

Attachment to what? The answer has been repeated over the past two and a half millennia by everyone from Buddhist teachers to the Dalai Lamas and Jedi Master Yoda. Before we delve too deeply into those answers, let's hear what Buddha has to say:

"See them, floundering in their sense of mine, like fish in the puddles of a dried-up stream — and, seeing this, live with no mine, not forming attachment for states of becoming."

This quote may seem a little confusing. But what religion isn't? After all, it took Buddha a few years before he finally realized what would set him apart from the common person: the ability to not get caught up in a dry stream. The dried-up stream is described by

Buddha as:

"There is no fear for one whose mind is not filled with desires."

Desires lead to attachments, and attachment, in turn, inevitably leads to human suffering. Sound familiar? If you've ever watched a Star Wars movie featuring any dialogue spoken by Yoda, you have probably heard the words said in reverse. If you're not a fan of Space Operas, then you might be surprised to know that one of the most popular film franchises contains a plethora of Buddhist teachings. For example, here is a quote from Yoda:

> *"Death is a natural part of life. Rejoice for those around you who transform into the Force. Mourn them do not. Miss them do not. Attachment leads to jealousy. The shadow of greed, that is."*

Obviously, Yoda didn't write this quote. A grey-haired man named George Lucas did because characters don't write themselves. However, Yoda is a carrier of Buddhist teachings in the Star Wars universe. So, technically speaking, old George Lucas didn't write it either. Buddha did. Through his search for enlightenment, the former rice farm aristocrat figured out the best way to fully awaken the mind; to let go of everything you hold dear, including the people you love. Yoda, in the same quote, goes on to say:

"Train yourself to let go of everything you fear to lose."

I never thought I would use a fictional character as a source, but Yoda is essentially regurgitating Buddha teachings. There is a reason both Jedis and Buddhist monks leave behind their possessions, swear a vow not to get married, and wear simple, long, matching robes. Lucas borrowed a lot from Buddha when creating the religion of the Jedi. Even sci-fi fans owe a lot to Buddha. But his followers are the ones who owe the most to Buddha's spiritual discovery.

Buddhist Practices and the Origins of Meditation

Millions, if not billions, have practiced Buddhism through the centuries, and all of them have at least learned what it takes, in Buddha's opinion, to achieve enlightenment. As you can see, actually achieving enlightenment was not something most people could or even wanted to do. The achievement requires you to detach yourself from human desires like love because loving someone can definitely lead to pain and suffering, as anyone who's ever had a pet before can fully comprehend. Nevertheless, Buddha calls for us to give that up, to detach from our loves and desires. Because once we let go of our attachments, worrying about the future, and dwelling on the past, we can live fully in the present and suffer no longer. The method, or practice, Buddha created to psychologically accomplish all this detachment is called meditation. Although there are several different forms of meditation that Buddhists practice, the style of meditation some sources champion over others is dhyana, a method that requires the practitioner to train their mind not to think. At first glance, this might sound impossible. But it is the primary way Buddha taught his followers to achieve a mental state called nirvana. No, not the awesome feeling you get when you listen to Kurt Cobain's awesome music. The mental state Buddha is referring to allows one to discard and sever themselves from their attachments and live free of pain and suffering.

Nowadays, everyone and their mom at least knows or is familiar with the practice of meditation. Even if they are practicing a different meditation form, they owe a lot to Buddha. He is essentially one of the inventors of mindfulness. While the science behind mindfulness and its perceived benefits is up for debate, the practice has touched almost everyone living on earth at some point in their lives, despite one of its pioneers having died almost 3 thousand years ago. Which brings us to...

Buddha's Death

Buddha's death is shrouded in several myths and his own twist on an ascension story. However, most early sources describe him as getting old like any other person, eventually dying in either 483 BCE or 400 BCE, living around 80 years old. He died as one would expect, while in nirvana, his spirit moving on to a state they would later call *Parinirvana*, the final rebirth and suffering after death. Some sources say that upon his death, the aging Buddha uttered the 4 dhyanas, the 4 immaterial impairments, and then died right on the 1st dhyana.

After his death, the followers of Buddha cremated his body and saved his remaining bones. They then took the bones and buried them in monuments all across Northern India as relics of their beloved teacher. Buddha's teachings only grew after his death, first spreading across India before making their way to China, then Japan, and in these modern times, all over the world.

Buddha shows that no matter your background or who your parents are defines what you have to do with your life. His teachings also offer much inspiration. As Buddha said:

> *"We are shaped by our thoughts; we become what we think. When the mind is pure, joy follows like a shadow that never leaves."*

Here are some final Buddha quotes:

> *"Pain is inevitable. Suffering is optional."*

> *"Don't rush anything. When the time is right it'll happen."*

"There are only two mistakes one can make along the road to truth; not going all the way, and not starting."

"One moment can change a day, one day can change a life, and one life can change the world."

"Quiet the mind and the soul will speak."

As a final request (if you haven't done so already), I have a small favor to ask. As a smaller author in a huge genre, I have learned that gathering reviews are hugely important to us.

If you like what you have read, and it has brought some value and perspective to your life, it would help me out immensely if you could take 30 seconds of your time and head over to amazon and write a nice brief review. A sentence or two will do!

Just scan the relevant QR code with your phone camera and it will take you straight there.

US: **UK:**

Thank you! I can't wait to see your thoughts.

CONCLUSION

So there we end. I hope this book fulfilled its purpose of making historical figures more relatable and accessible. It was a thoroughly enjoyable experience researching and putting together this series. I learned so much myself. With the range of unique characters contained in this book, I hope at least one or two made a positive impact on you and inspired you to take some action in your life. These people grew up in different worlds to you and me, many of whom changed the game in whatever field or area of expertise they were involved in.

Sir John Franklin's curiosity and explorer instincts may have led to his eventual disappearance and death, but he inspired and paved the way for the next crop of Arctic and Antarctic explorers, like Roald Amundsen (series 2), who was the first man to complete the journey of the Northwest Passage, linking the Atlantic Ocean with the Pacific.

Socrates, the ancient Greek philosopher, may have never been heard of were it not for his student Plato (series 2), who recited all his work and spread his teachings. Freud's theories may have been seen as outlandish and ridiculous, but he founded psychoanalysis, which essentially led to what we know today as therapy. His work was continued and upgraded by his successor Carl Yung, a man whose work is regularly mentioned by Jordan Peterson.

Cleopatra showed incredible attributes and resilience as a female emperor in a time of male-dominated ones. Da

Vinci and Mozart used their creative talents in art and music to inspire generations to come. Charles Ponzi may have been a crook, but he forced security forces to up their game in identifying all types of fraud. Was it not for Emmeline Pankhurst's sheer grit and determination, for how long more would women's rights have been ignored? The list goes on.

We all face challenges in our lives, no matter how big or small they seem. The world is evolving at a frightening pace, with many distractions capable of putting you off path. There is not one person in history that didn't face huge adversities and setbacks. But they never gave up. Whatever your goal is, just remember that tomorrow is always a new day, a fresh start. As Mahatma Gandhi famously said:

"Each night, when I go to sleep, I die. And the next morning, when I wake up, I am reborn."

BONUS QUIZ

To test your memory and refresh your knowledge on the characters in this book, I have attached this bonus quiz section. It contains 20 quotes where you have to try and guess who said each quote with multiple choice answers. Feel free to ask family members or friends to join in. Good luck.

Question 1

Who does this philosophical quote belong to?

"To go wrong in one's own way is better than to go right in someone else's."

A) Mahatma Gandhi

B) Sigmund Freud

C) Fyodor Dostoevsky

D) Socrates

Question 2

This powerful quote about strength, comes from which great mind?

"Out of your vulnerabilities will come your strength."

A) Buddha

B) Fyodor Dostoevsky

C) Mahatma Gandhi

D) Sigmund Freud

Question 3

Who does this pondering quote about the universe belong to?

> *"Gravity explains the motions of the planets, but it cannot explain who sets the planets in motion."*

A) Leonardo Da Vinci
B) Isaac Newton
C) Albert Einstein
D) Socrates

Question 4

Which great warrior said the following?

> *"Treat your men as you would your own beloved sons. And they will follow you into the deepest valley."*

A) Sun Tzu
B) Genghis Khan
C) Joan of Arc
D) Julius Caesar

Question 5

Who said this quote as. Demonstration of their fighting spirit?

> *"I will not be triumphed over"*

A) Julius Caesar
B) Joan of Arc

C) Genghis Khan
D) Cleopatra

Question 6

Which historical figure gave this explanation about the reality of the work of genius?

> *"Genius is one percent inspiration and ninety-nine percent perspiration."*

A) Albert Einstein
B) Thomas Edison
C) Leonardo Da Vinci
D) Wolfgang Amadeus Mozart

Question 7

Who did this Religious quote come from?
> *"Trust in God - she will provide."*

A) Cleopatra
B) Joan of Arc
C) Emmeline Pankhurst
D) Jesus Christ

Question 8

This famous quote is from which historical figure?

> *"An eye for eye only ends up making the whole world blind."*

A) Socrates
B) Buddha

C) Jesus Christ

D) Mahatma Gandhi

Question 9

Who said this line about breaking the law?

"If you must break the law, do it to seize power: in all other cases observe it."

A) Julius Caesar

B) Sun Tzu

C) Emmeline Pankhurst

D) Joan of Arc

Question 10

Which great mind said this thought provoking sentence?

"He who is not contented with what he has, would not be contented with what he would like to have."

A) Socrates

B) Fyodor Dostoevsky

C) Buddha

D) Sigmund Freud

Question 11

Which fearless warrior said this famous line?

"I am the punishment of God"

A) Leif Erikson

B) Joan of Arc

C) Genghis Khan

D) Julius Caesar

Question 12

Which genius mind had this to say about learning?

"Learning never exhausts the mind"

A) Leonardo Da Vinci

B) Thomas Edison

C) Albert Einstein

D) Isaac Newton

Question 13

Who had this to say about the power of the mind in war?

"All battles are first won or lost in the mind"

A) Genghis Khan

B) Julius Caesar

C) Joan of Arc

D) Sun Tzu

Question 14

Who said this piece of wisdom about life?

"It is more blessed to give than to receive"

A) Socrates

B) Buddha

C) Mahatma Gandhi

D) Jesus Christ

Question 15

Who had this to say about warfare?

> *"Let your plans be dark and impenetrable as night, and when you move, fall like a thunderbolt."*

A) Leif Erikson
B) Genghis Khan
C) Sun Tzu
D) Joan of Arc

Question 16

Who had this to say about the mind and the soul?
"Quiet the mind and the soul will speak."

A) Fyodor Dostoevsky
B) Socrates
C) Sigmund Freud
D) Buddha

Question 17

Which historical figure had this to say about his place in history?
"I start where the last man left off."

A) Thomas Edison
B) Albert Einstein
C) Leonardo Da Vinci
D) Isaac Newton

Question 18

Who had this to say about their dreams of success?
"I landed in this country with $2.50 in cash and $1 million in hopes, and those hopes never left me."

- A) Leonardo Da Vinci
- B) Thomas Edison
- C) Julius Caesar
- D) Charles Ponzi

Question 19

This famous line was said by which great mind?
"Strong minds discuss ideas, average minds discuss events, weak minds discuss people."

A) Fyodor Dostoevsky
B) Sigmund Freud
C) Socrates
D) Joan of Arc

Question 20

Which historical character from this book said this line?
"Yes, but I too had to work in order that I might be exempt from work now."

- A) Albert Einstein
- B) Leonardo Da Vinci
- C) Wolfgang Amadeus Mozart
- D) Thomas Edison

THE ANSWERS:

Question 1 The answer is: C) Fyodor Dostoevsky

Question 2 The answer is: D) Sigmund Freud

Question 3 The answer is: B) Isaac Newton,

Question 4 The answer is: A) Sun Tzu

Question 5 The answer is: D) Cleopatra

Question 6 The answer is: B) Thomas Edison

Question 7 The answer is: C) Emmeline Pankhurst

Question 8 The answer is: D) Mahatma Gandhi

Question 9 The answer is: A) Julius Caesar

Question 10 The answer is: A) Socrates

Question 11 The answer is: C) Genghis Khan

Question 12 The answer is: A) Leonardo Da Vinci

Question 13 The answer is: C) Joan of Arc

Question 14 The answer is: D) Jesus Christ

Question 15 The answer is: C) Sun Tzu

Question 16 The answer is: D) Buddha

Question 17 The answer is: A) Thomas Edison

Question 18 The answer is: D) Charles Ponzi

Question 19 The answer is: C) Socrates

Question 20 The answer is: B) Mozart

REFERENCES

A&E Networks Television. (2021, May 3). *Sigmund Freud.* Biography.com. Retrieved February 23, 2022, from https://www.biography.com/scholar/sigmund-freud

Access your bible from anywhere. BibleGateway.com: A searchable online Bible in over 150 versions and 50 languages. (n.d.). Retrieved February 23, 2022, from https://www.biblegateway.com/

Barton, B. (2000). *The Man Nobody Knows: A discovery of the real jesus.* I.R. Dee.

Beardsley, M. (2002). *Deadly winter: The life of sir John Franklin.* Chatham.
Beliefnet, & Editor, B. (2021, August 10). *6 practical life lessons jesus taught the disciples.* Beliefnet. Retrieved February 23, 2022, from https://www.beliefnet.com/faiths/christianity/6-practical-life-lessons-jesus-taught-the-disciples.aspx

Biography – Franklin, sir John – Volume VII (1836-1850) – dictionary of Canadian biography. Home – Dictionary of Canadian Biography. (n.d.). Retrieved February 23, 2022, from
http://www.biographi.ca/en/bio/franklin_john_7E.html

Branscomb, B. H. (1967). *The gospel of mark*. Hodder and Stoughton.

Brown, D. A. (1999). *Leonardo da Vinci: Origins of a genius*. Yale University Press.

Carrithers, M. (2011). The buddha: A very short introduction. Oxford University Press.

Category:John Franklin. Wikimedia Commons. (n.d.). Retrieved February 24, 2022, from https://commons.wikimedia.org/wiki/Category:John_Franklin

Center, S. L. (2015, February 10). *Thomas Edison's inventive life*. Lemelson Center for the Study of Invention and Innovation. Retrieved February 23, 2022, from https://invention.si.edu/thomas-edisons-inventive-life

Discover walks blog. (n.d.). Retrieved February 23, 2022, from https://www.discoverwalks.com/blog/

E., K. D. E. (2009). *Cleopatra and Rome*. Belknap Press of Harvard University Press.
Encyclopædia Britannica, inc. (n.d.). Encyclopædia Britannica. Retrieved February 23, 2022, from https://www.britannica.com/

File:Emmeline Pankhurst, seated (1913).JPG - wikipedia. (n.d.). Retrieved February 24, 2022, from https://en.wikipedia.org/wiki/File:Emmeline_Pankhurst,_seated_(1913).jpg

File:Leif Erikson Statue, Duluth (15290644106).JPG ... (n.d.). Retrieved February 24, 2022, from

https://commons.wikimedia.org/wiki/File:Leif_Erikson_S
tatue,_Duluth_(15290644106).jpg

File:Ponzi1920.jpg - Wikipedia republished // Wiki 2. -
Wikipedia Republished // WIKI 2. (n.d.). Retrieved
February 24, 2022, from
https://wiki2.org/en/File:Ponzi1920_jpg

Gandhi, M. K., & Jack, H. A. (2003). *The Gandhi reader: A
sourcebook of his life and writings.* Grove Press.
Goldsworthy, A. K. (2008). *Caesar. ; life of a Colossus.* Yale
University Press.
Goodreads. (n.d.). *Popular quotes.* Goodreads. Retrieved
February 23, 2022, from
https://www.goodreads.com/quotes

Harpercollins. (1995, January 31). *Mozart : Maynard Solomon :
Free download, Borrow, and streaming.* Internet Archive.
Retrieved February 23, 2022, from
https://archive.org/details/mozartlife00solo

Hirakawa, A., & Groner, P. (1989, December 31). A history
of Indian buddhism : From śākyamuni to early mahāyāna.
ScholarSpace at University of Hawaii at Manoa: Home.

Home. (n.d.). Retrieved February 23, 2022, from
https://www.loc.gov/static/collections/edison-company-
motion-pictures-and-sound-recordings/articles-and-
essays/biography/life-of-thomas-alva-edison.html

Ingstad, H., & Ingstad, A. S. (2001). *The Viking Discovery of
America: The excavation of a Norse settlement in L'Anse aux
Meadows, Newfoundland.* Checkmark Books.

Isaacson, W. (2017). *Einstein: His life and universe.* Simon &
Schuster.

Join 175,523,040 academics and researchers. Academia.edu - Share research. (n.d.). Retrieved February 23, 2022, from https://www.academia.edu/

Kjetsaa, G. (1989). *Fyodor Dostoyevsky, a writer's life.* Fawcett Columbine.

Knapp, A. (2021, December 10). *Nikola Tesla wasn't god and Thomas Edison wasn't the devil.* Forbes. Retrieved February 23, 2022, from https://www.forbes.com/sites/alexknapp/2012/05/18/nikola-tesla-wasnt-god-and-thomas-edison-wasnt-the-devil/?sh=71b39321a21a

Mental floss. Mental Floss. (n.d.). Retrieved February 23, 2022, from https://www.mentalfloss.com/

Morrison, D. R. (2011). *The cambridge companion to socrates.* Cambridge University Press.

Mozart, W. A., & Spaethling, R. (2000). *Selected letters.* W.W. Norton.

New York : Random House. (1980, January 1). *Freud, the man and the cause : Clark, Ronald William : Free Download, borrow, and streaming.* Internet Archive. Retrieved February 23, 2022, from https://archive.org/details/freudmancause00clar

New York : Scribner. (1977, January 1). *Jesus : An historian's review of the gospels : Grant, Michael, 1914-2004 : Free Download, borrow, and streaming.* Internet Archive. Retrieved February 23, 2022, from https://archive.org/details/jesushistoriansr00gran/page/n11/mode/2up

New York, NY : Harper. (1970, January 1). *Joan of arc : A history : Castor, Helen : Free download, borrow, and streaming.*

Internet Archive. Retrieved February 23, 2022, from https://archive.org/details/joanofarchistory0000cast_n6r7

Penner, H. H. (2009). *Rediscovering the buddha: Legends of the buddha and their interpretation.* Oxford University Press.

Pugh, M. (2013). *The Pankhursts: The history of one radical family.* Vintage Digital.
Ratchnevsky, P., & Haining, T. N. (2006). *Genghis Khan: His life and legacy.* Blackwell Publishing.
Retrieved February 22, 2022, from https://scholarspace.manoa.hawaii.edu/handle/10125/230 30

Richard MAHONEY - r dot mahoney at indica-et-buddhica dot org. (n.d.). *The dating of the historical buddha: A review article.* INDOLOGY RSS 10. Retrieved February 23, 2022, from https://web.archive.org/web/20110226184207/http://ind ology.info/papers/cousins/

Sawyer, R. D., & Sawyer Mei-chün. (2007). *The Seven Military Classics of Ancient China: Including the Art of War = Wu Jing Qi Shu.* BasicBooks.

Seaver, K. A. (1998). *The frozen echo: Greenland and the exploration of North America, C. A.D. 1000-1500.* Stanford University Press.

Siametis, C. (2018, September 1). *Socrates: The simplicity of the Wisdom.* Greeks Channel. Retrieved February 24, 2022, from https://www.greekschannel.com/socrates-the-simplicity-of-the-wisdom/

Sigmund Freud: Life, theory & contributions to psychology - free essay example. PapersOwl.com. (2020, June 11). Retrieved February 23, 2022, from https://papersowl.com/examples/sigmund-freud-life-theory-contributions-to-psychology/

Stanley, M. (2019, May 23). *The man who made einstein world-famous*. BBC News. Retrieved February 23, 2022, from https://www.bbc.com/news/science-environment-48369980

Taylor, J., & Taylor, J. (1978). *The Bible*. Printed by Fay & Davison.

The latest from history. All articles | Sky HISTORY UK TV Channel. (n.d.). Retrieved February 23, 2022, from https://www.history.co.uk/articles

Thomas A. Edison quote: "everyone steals in commerce and industry. I've stolen a lot, myself. but I know how to steal! they don't know how to Ste...". Quotefancy. (n.d.). Retrieved February 23, 2022, from https://quotefancy.com/quote/916668/Thomas-A-Edison-Everyone-steals-in-commerce-and-industry-I-ve-stolen-a-lot-myself-But-I

Todorovic, A., Greensboro, U. N. C., King, B., jasminejames536, King, B., Pietrowski, J., Manning, A., Martin, C., Unique, E., Robinson, A., Patterson, K., Hamschin, H., Davis, M., Calle, J., & Cummings, L. (2019, October 17). *Why it's better to be a Tesla than an Edison*. The Odyssey Online. Retrieved February 23, 2022, from https://www.theodysseyonline.com/tesla-edison

Tzu, S. (2009). *The art of war*. Pax Librorum.

University of Minnesota Press. (1999, January 1). *The interrogation of Joan of arc : Karen Sullivan : Free Download, borrow, and streaming*. Internet Archive. Retrieved February 23, 2022, from https://archive.org/details/interrogationofj00sull

Westfall, R. S. (2015). *The life of Isaac Newton*. Cambridge University Press.

Wikimedia Foundation. (2022, February 1). *Main page.* Wikipedia. Retrieved February 23, 2022, from https://www.wikipedia.org/

Wikimedia Foundation. (2022, February 20). *Sun Tzu image.* Wikipedia. Retrieved February 24, 2022, from https://en.wikipedia.org/wiki/Sun_Tzu

Wikimedia Foundation. (2022, January 29). *Julius Caesar.* Wikipedia. Retrieved February 23, 2022, from https://en.wikipedia.org/wiki/Julius_Caesar

Xplore. (n.d.). *Inspirational quotes at brainyquote.* BrainyQuote. Retrieved February 23, 2022, from https://www.brainyquote.com/

Zuckoff, M. (2006*). Ponzi's scheme: The true story of a financial legend.* Random House.

ABOUT AUTHOR

Patrick Marcus is a young Irish independent author and self-publisher. He is also a former high school teacher with undergraduate and post-graduate first-class honors degrees. With 12 years' experience in the history industry, Patricks initial interest in historical figures came from his father who was always talking about them and had a vast number of books and VCRs/DVDs lying around their house growing up. Patrick would then do his own research reading books and watching videos and documentaries on these characters to discover just how interesting their lives really were. Patrick has also been writing as a freelancer for many years, writing many articles and pieces on all things history.